(ex·ploring)

1. Investigating in a systematic way: examining. 2. Searching into or ranging over for the purpose of discovery.

Getting Started with

Microsoft® Outlook® 2016

Series Editor Mary Anne Poatsy

Barbara Stover

Series Created by Dr. Robert T. Grauer

330 Hudson Street, NY, NY 10013

Vice President of IT & Career Skills: Andrew Gilfillan
Senior Portfolio Manager: Samantha Lewis
Team Lead, Project Management: Laura Burgess
Project Manager: Barbara Stover
Development Editor: Barbara Stover
Editorial Assistant: Michael Campbell
Director of Product Marketing: Maggie Waples
Director of Field Marketing: Leigh Ann Sims
Product Marketing Manager: Kaylee Carlson
Field Marketing Managers: Molly Schmidt & Joanna Conley
Senior Operations Specialist: Maura Zaldivar-Garcia
Interior and Cover Design: Cenveo
Senior Product Model Manager: Eric Hakanson
Production and Digital Studio Lead: Heather Darby
Media Producer, MyITLab: Jaimie Noy
Course Producer, MyITLab: Amanda Losonsky
Digital Project Manager, MyITLab: Becca Lowe
Media Project Manager, Production: John Cassar
Full-Service Project Management: iEnergizer Aptara®, Ltd.
Composition: iEnergizer Aptara®, Ltd.
Cover Image Credits: cunico/Fotolia (compass rose); mawrhis/Fotolia (checker pattern); wavebreakmedia/Shutterstock (students); Sergey Nivens/Fotolia (world); dotshock/Shutterstock (business people)

Credits and acknowledgments borrowed from other sources and reproduced, with permission, in this textbook appear on the appropriate page within text.

Microsoft and/or its respective suppliers make no representations about the suitability of the information contained in the documents and related graphics published as part of the services for any purpose. All such documents and related graphics are provided "as is" without warranty of any kind. Microsoft and/or its respective suppliers hereby disclaim all warranties and conditions with regard to this information, including all warranties and conditions of merchantability, whether express, implied or statutory, fitness for a particular purpose, title and non-infringement. In no event shall Microsoft and/or its respective suppliers be liable for any special, indirect or consequential damages or any damages whatsoever resulting from loss of use, data or profits, whether in an action of contract, negligence or other tortious action, arising out of or in connection with the use or performance of information available from the services.

The documents and related graphics contained herein could include technical inaccuracies or typographical errors. Changes are periodically added to the information herein. Microsoft and/or its respective suppliers may make improvements and/or changes in the product(s) and/or the program(s) described herein at any time. Partial screen shots may be viewed in full within the software version specified.

Microsoft® and Windows® are registered trademarks of the Microsoft Corporation in the U.S.A. and other countries. This book is not sponsored or endorsed by or affiliated with the Microsoft Corporation.

Copyright © 2017 by Pearson Education, Inc. All rights reserved. Manufactured in the United States of America. This publication is protected by copyright and permission should be obtained from the publisher prior to any prohibited reproduction, storage in a retrieval system, or transmission in any form or by any means, electronic, mechanical, photocopying, recording, or likewise. For information regarding permissions, request forms and the appropriate contacts within the Pearson Education Global Rights & Permissions department, please visit www.pearsoned.com/permissions/.

Many of the designations by manufacturers and sellers to distinguish their products are claimed as trademarks. Where those designations appear in this book, and the publisher was aware of a trademark claim, the designations have been printed in initial caps or all caps.

Cataloging-in-Publication data is on file with the Library of Congress.

3 18

ISBN 10:   0-13-449760-0
ISBN 13: 978-0-13-449760-0

About the Authors

Mary Anne Poatsy, Series Editor

Mary Anne is a senior faculty member at Montgomery County Community College, teaching various computer application and concepts courses in face-to-face and online environments. She holds a B.A. in Psychology and Education from Mount Holyoke College and an M.B.A. in Finance from Northwestern University's Kellogg Graduate School of Management.

Mary Anne has more than 18 years of educational experience. She is currently adjunct faculty at Montgomery County Community College. She has also taught at Gywnedd Mercy University, Bucks County Community College, and Muhlenberg College, as well as conducted personal training. Before teaching, she was Vice President at Shearson Lehman in the Municipal Bond Investment Banking Department.

Barbara Stover, Outlook Author

Barbara's professional life is focused on education. As a professor at Marion Technical College in Marion, Ohio, she taught Microsoft Office applications and Web technologies. She serves as an adjunct faculty member at George Washington University in Washington D.C., in the Educational Technology Leadership Masters degree program. She has authored several textbooks and edited many others.

Dedications

For my husband, Ted, who unselfishly continues to take on more than his share to support me throughout the process; and for my children, Laura, Carolyn, and Teddy, whose encouragement and love have been inspiring.

Mary Anne Poatsy

To you, the student, embarking on the adventure of a lifetime—your career. Wishing you success!

Barbara Stover

Contents

Microsoft Outlook 2016

CHAPTER ONE Introduction to Outlook: Managing Email, Contacts, Tasks, and Calendars   2

CASE STUDY T-SHIRTS TO GO	2
INTRODUCTION TO OUTLOOK AND EMAIL	4
Identifying the Components of the Outlook Window	4
Managing Email	9
HANDS-ON EXERCISE 1:	
Introduction to Outlook and Email	20
OUTLOOK CONTACTS	30
Managing Contacts	30
HANDS-ON EXERCISE 2:	
Outlook Contacts	35
OUTLOOK CALENDAR, TASK LIST, AND NOTES	42
Managing the Outlook Calendar	42
Managing Tasks and Notes	45
HANDS-ON EXERCISE 3:	
Outlook Calendar, Task List, and Notes	48
CHAPTER OBJECTIVES REVIEW	53
KEY TERMS MATCHING	55
MULTIPLE CHOICE	56
PRACTICE EXERCISES	57
MID-LEVEL EXERCISES	62
BEYOND THE CLASSROOM	65
CAPSTONE EXERCISE	66
GLOSSARY	68
INDEX	69

Acknowledgments

The Exploring team acknowledges and thanks all the reviewers who helped us throughout the years by providing us with their invaluable comments, suggestions, and constructive criticism.

Adriana Lumpkin
Midland College

Alan S. Abrahams
Virginia Tech

Alexandre C. Probst
Colorado Christian University

Ali Berrached
University of Houston–Downtown

Allen Alexander
Delaware Technical & Community College

Andrea Marchese
Maritime College, State University of New York

Andrew Blitz
Broward College; Edison State College

Angel Norman
University of Tennessee, Knoxville

Angela Clark
University of South Alabama

Ann Rovetto
Horry-Georgetown Technical College

Astrid Todd
Guilford Technical Community College

Audrey Gillant
Maritime College, State University of New York

Barbara Stover
Marion Technical College

Barbara Tollinger
Sinclair Community College

Ben Brahim Taha
Auburn University

Beverly Amer
Northern Arizona University

Beverly Fite
Amarillo College

Biswadip Ghosh
Metropolitan State University of Denver

Bonita Volker
Tidewater Community College

Bonnie Homan
San Francisco State University

Brad West
Sinclair Community College

Brian Powell
West Virginia University

Carol Buser
Owens Community College

Carol Roberts
University of Maine

Carolyn Barren
Macomb Community College

Carolyn Borne
Louisiana State University

Cathy Poyner
Truman State University

Charles Hodgson
Delgado Community College

Chen Zhang
Bryant University

Cheri Higgins
Illinois State University

Cheryl Brown
Delgado Community College

Cheryl Hinds
Norfolk State University

Cheryl Sypniewski
Macomb Community College

Chris Robinson
Northwest State Community College

Cindy Herbert
Metropolitan Community College–Longview

Craig J. Peterson
American InterContinental University

Dana Hooper
University of Alabama

Dana Johnson
North Dakota State University

Daniela Marghitu
Auburn University

David Noel
University of Central Oklahoma

David Pulis
Maritime College, State University of New York

David Thornton
Jacksonville State University

Dawn Medlin
Appalachian State University

Debby Keen
University of Kentucky

Debra Chapman
University of South Alabama

Debra Hoffman
Southeast Missouri State University

Derrick Huang
Florida Atlantic University

Diana Baran
Henry Ford Community College

Diane Cassidy
The University of North Carolina at Charlotte

Diane L. Smith
Henry Ford Community College

Dick Hewer
Ferris State College

Don Danner
San Francisco State University

Don Hoggan
Solano College

Don Riggs
SUNY Schenectady County Community College

Doncho Petkov
Eastern Connecticut State University

Donna Ehrhart
State University of New York at Brockport

Elaine Crable
Xavier University

Elizabeth Duett
Delgado Community College

Erhan Uskup
Houston Community College–Northwest

Eric Martin
University of Tennessee

Erika Nadas
Wilbur Wright College

Floyd Winters
Manatee Community College

Frank Lucente
Westmoreland County Community College

G. Jan Wilms
Union University

Gail Cope
Sinclair Community College

Gary DeLorenzo
California University of Pennsylvania

Gary Garrison
Belmont University

Gary McFall
Purdue University

George Cassidy
Sussex County Community College

Gerald Braun
Xavier University

Gerald Burgess
Western New Mexico University

Gladys Swindler
Fort Hays State University

Hector Frausto
California State University Los Angeles

Heith Hennel
Valencia Community College

Henry Rudzinski
Central Connecticut State University

Irene Joos
La Roche College

Iwona Rusin
Baker College; Davenport University

J. Roberto Guzman
San Diego Mesa College

Jacqueline D. Lawson
Henry Ford Community College

Jakie Brown Jr.
Stevenson University

James Brown
Central Washington University

James Powers
University of Southern Indiana

Jane Stam
Onondaga Community College

Janet Bringhurst
Utah State University

Jean Welsh
Lansing Community College

Jeanette Dix
Ivy Tech Community College

Jennifer Day
Sinclair Community College

Jill Canine
Ivy Tech Community College

Jill Young
Southeast Missouri State University

Jim Chaffee
The University of Iowa Tippie College of Business

Joanne Lazirko
University of Wisconsin–Milwaukee

Jodi Milliner
Kansas State University

John Hollenbeck
Blue Ridge Community College

John Seydel
Arkansas State University

Judith A. Scheeren
Westmoreland County Community College

Judith Brown
The University of Memphis

Juliana Cypert
Tarrant County College

Kamaljeet Sanghera
George Mason University

Karen Priestly
Northern Virginia Community College

Karen Ravan
Spartanburg Community College

Karen Tracey
Central Connecticut State University

Kathleen Brenan
Ashland University

Ken Busbee
Houston Community College

Kent Foster
Winthrop University

Kevin Anderson
Solano Community College

Kim Wright
The University of Alabama

Kristen Hockman
University of Missouri–Columbia

Kristi Smith
Allegany College of Maryland

Laura Marcoulides
Fullerton College

Laura McManamon
University of Dayton

Laurence Boxer
Niagara University

Leanne Chun
Leeward Community College

Lee McClain
Western Washington University

Linda D. Collins
Mesa Community College

Linda Johnsonius
Murray State University

Linda Lau
Longwood University

Linda Theus
Jackson State Community College

Linda Williams
Marion Technical College

Lisa Miller
University of Central Oklahoma

Lister Horn
Pensacola Junior College

Lixin Tao
Pace University

Loraine Miller
Cayuga Community College

Lori Kielty
Central Florida Community College

Lorna Wells
Salt Lake Community College

Lorraine Sauchin
Duquesne University

Lucy Parakhovnik
California State University, Northridge

Lynn Keane
University of South Carolina

Lynn Mancini
Delaware Technical Community College

Mackinzee Escamilla
South Plains College

Marcia Welch
Highline Community College

Margaret McManus
Northwest Florida State College

Margaret Warrick
Allan Hancock College

Marilyn Hibbert
Salt Lake Community College

Mark Choman
Luzerne County Community College

Maryann Clark
University of New Hampshire

Mary Beth Tarver
Northwestern State University

Mary Duncan
University of Missouri–St. Louis

Melissa Nemeth
Indiana University-Purdue University Indianapolis

Melody Alexander
Ball State University

Michael Douglas
University of Arkansas at Little Rock

Michael Dunklebarger
Alamance Community College

Michael G. Skaff
College of the Sequoias

Michele Budnovitch
Pennsylvania College of Technology

Mike Jochen
East Stroudsburg University

Mike Michaelson
Palomar College

Mike Scroggins
Missouri State University

Mimi Spain
Southern Maine Community College

Muhammed Badamas
Morgan State University

NaLisa Brown
University of the Ozarks

Nancy Grant
Community College of Allegheny
County–South Campus

Nanette Lareau
University of Arkansas Community
College–Morrilton

Nikia Robinson
Indian River State University

Pam Brune
Chattanooga State Community College

Pam Uhlenkamp
Iowa Central Community College

Patrick Smith
Marshall Community and Technical College

Paul Addison
Ivy Tech Community College

Paula Ruby
Arkansas State University

Peggy Burrus
Red Rocks Community College

Peter Ross
SUNY Albany

Philip H. Nielson
Salt Lake Community College

Philip Valvalides
Guilford Technical Community College

Ralph Hooper
University of Alabama

Ranette Halverson
Midwestern State University

Richard Blamer
John Carroll University

Richard Cacace
Pensacola Junior College

Richard Hewer
Ferris State University

Richard Sellers
Hill College

Rob Murray
Ivy Tech Community College

Robert Banta
Macomb Community College

Robert Dušek
Northern Virginia Community College

Robert G. Phipps Jr.
West Virginia University

Robert Sindt
Johnson County Community College

Robert Warren
Delgado Community College

Rocky Belcher
Sinclair Community College

Roger Pick
University of Missouri at Kansas City

Ronnie Creel
Troy University

Rosalie Westerberg
Clover Park Technical College

Ruth Neal
Navarro College

Sandra Thomas
Troy University

Sheila Gionfriddo
Luzerne County Community College

Sherrie Geitgey
Northwest State Community College

Sherry Lenhart
Terra Community College

Sophia Wilberscheid
Indian River State College

Sophie Lee
California State University, Long Beach

Stacy Johnson
Iowa Central Community College

Stephanie Kramer
Northwest State Community College

Stephen Z. Jourdan
Auburn University at Montgomery

Steven Schwarz
Raritan Valley Community College

Sue A. McCrory
Missouri State University

Sumathy Chandrashekar
Salisbury University

Susan Fuschetto
Cerritos College

Susan Medlin
UNC Charlotte

Susan N. Dozier
Tidewater Community College

Suzan Spitzberg
Oakton Community College

Suzanne M. Jeska
County College of Morris

Sven Aelterman
Troy University

Sy Hirsch
Sacred Heart University

Sylvia Brown
Midland College

Tanya Patrick
Clackamas Community College

Terri Holly
Indian River State College

Terry Ray Rigsby
Hill College

Thomas Rienzo
Western Michigan University

Tina Johnson
Midwestern State University

Tommy Lu
Delaware Technical Community College

Troy S. Cash
Northwest Arkansas Community College

Vicki Robertson
Southwest Tennessee Community

Vickie Pickett
Midland College

Weifeng Chen
California University of Pennsylvania

Wes Anthony
Houston Community College

William Ayen
University of Colorado at Colorado Springs

Wilma Andrews
Virginia Commonwealth University

Yvonne Galusha
University of Iowa

Acknowledgments

Special thanks to our content development and technical team:

Barbara Stover   Patti Hammerle
Julie Boyles   Susan Fry

Preface

The Exploring Series and You

Exploring is Pearson's Office Application series that requires students like you to think "beyond the point and click." In this edition, we have worked to restructure the Exploring experience around the way you, today's modern student, actually use your resources.

The goal of Exploring is, as it has always been, to go farther than teaching just the steps to accomplish a task—the series provides the theoretical foundation for you to understand when and why to apply a skill. As a result, you achieve a deeper understanding of each application and can apply this critical thinking beyond Office and the classroom.

The How & Why of This Revision

Outcomes matter. Whether it's getting a good grade in this course, learning how to use Microsoft Office and Windows 10 so students can be successful in other courses, or learning a specific skill that will make learners successful in a future job, everyone has an outcome in mind. And outcomes matter. That is why we revised our chapter opener to focus on the outcomes students will achieve by working through each Exploring chapter. These are coupled with objectives and skills, providing a map students can follow to get everything they need from each chapter.

Critical Thinking and Collaboration are essential 21st-century skills. Students want and need to be successful in their future careers—so we used motivating case studies to show relevance of these skills to future careers.

Students today read, prepare, and study differently than students used to. Students use textbooks like a tool—they want to easily identify what they need to know and learn it efficiently. We have added key features, such as Tasks Lists (in purple) and Step Icons, and tracked everything via page numbers that allow efficient navigation, creating a map students can easily follow.

Students are exposed to technology. The new edition of Exploring moves beyond the basics of the software at a faster pace, without sacrificing coverage of the fundamental skills that students need to know.

Students are diverse. Students can be any age, any gender, any race, with any level of ability or learning style. With this in mind, we broadened our definition of "student resources" to include MyITLab, the most powerful and most ADA-compliant online homework and assessment tool around with a direct 1:1 content match with the Exploring Series. Exploring will be accessible to all students, regardless of learning style.

Providing You with a Map to Success to Move Beyond the Point and Click

All of these changes and additions will provide students an easy and efficient path to follow to be successful in this course, regardless of where they start at the beginning of this course. Our goal is to keep students engaged in both the hands-on and conceptual sides, helping achieve a higher level of understanding that will guarantee success in this course and in a future career.

In addition to the vision and experience of the series creator, Robert T. Grauer, we have assembled a tremendously talented team of Office Applications authors who have devoted themselves to teaching the ins and outs of Microsoft Word, Excel, Access, and PowerPoint. Led in this edition by series editor Mary Anne Poatsy, the whole team is dedicated to the Exploring mission of moving students **beyond the point and click**.

Key Features

The **How/Why Approach** helps students move beyond the point and click to a true understanding of how to apply Microsoft Office skills.

- **White Pages/Yellow Pages** clearly distinguish the theory (white pages) from the skills covered in the Hands-On Exercises (yellow pages) so students always know what they are supposed to be doing and why.
- **Case Study** presents a scenario for the chapter, creating a story that ties the Hands-On Exercises together.

The **Outcomes focus** allows students and instructors to know the higher-level learning goals and how those are achieved through discreet objectives and skills.

- **Outcomes** presented at the beginning of each chapter identify the learning goals for students and instructors.
- **Enhanced Objective Mapping** enables students to follow a directed path through each chapter, from the objectives list at the chapter opener through the exercises at the end of the chapter.
    - **Objectives List:** This provides a simple list of key objectives covered in the chapter. This includes page numbers so students can skip between objectives where they feel they need the most help.
    - **Step Icons:** These icons appear in the white pages and reference the step numbers in the Hands-On Exercises, providing a correlation between the two so students can easily find conceptual help when they are working hands-on and need a refresher.
    - **Quick Concepts Check:** A series of questions that appear briefly at the end of each white page section. These questions cover the most essential concepts in the white pages required for students to be successful in working the Hands-On Exercises. Page numbers are included for easy reference to help students locate the answers.
    - **Chapter Objectives Review:** Appears toward the end of the chapter and reviews all important concepts throughout the chapter. Newly designed in an easy-to-read bulleted format.

End-of-Chapter Exercises offer instructors several options for assessment. Each chapter has approximately 11–12 exercises ranging from multiple choice questions to open-ended projects.

- **Multiple Choice, Key Terms Matching, Practice Exercises, Mid-Level Exercises, Beyond the Classroom Exercises, and Capstone Exercises** appear at the end of all chapters.

Resources

Instructor Resources

The Instructor's Resource Center, available at **www.pearsonhighered.com**, includes the following:

- **Instructor Manual** provides one-stop-shop for instructors, including an overview of all available resources, teaching tips, as well as student data and solution files for every exercise.
- **Solution Files with Scorecards** assist with grading the Hands-On Exercises and end-of-chapter exercises.
- **Prepared Exams** allow instructors to assess all skills covered in a chapter with a single project.
- **Rubrics** for Mid-Level Creative Cases and Beyond the Classroom Cases in Microsoft Word format enable instructors to customize the assignments for their classes.
- **PowerPoint Presentations** with notes for each chapter are included for out-of-class study or review.
- **Multiple Choice, Key Term Matching, and Quick Concepts Check Answer Keys**
- **Test Bank** provides objective-based questions for every chapter.
- **Scripted Lectures** offer an in-class lecture guide for instructors to mirror the Hands-On Exercises.
- **Syllabus Templates**
  - Outcomes, Objectives, and Skills List
  - Assignment Sheet
  - File Guide

Student Resources

Student Data Files

Access your student data files needed to complete the exercises in this textbook at **www.pearsonhighered.com/exploring.**

Available in MyITLab

- **PowerPoints** provide a lecture review of the chapter content, and include narration.
- **Multiple Choice quizzes** enable you to test concepts you have learned by answering auto-graded questions.
- **eText** available in some MyITLab courses and includes links to videos, student data files, and other learning aids.
- **Key Terms** quizzes enable you to test your understanding of key terms in each chapter.

1. Investigating in a systematic way: examining. 2. Searching into or ranging over for the purpose of discovery.

Getting Started with

Microsoft® Outlook® 2016

Outlook

Introduction to Outlook

LEARNING OBJECTIVE You will effectively communicate using email, and manage contacts, tasks, and calendars.

OBJECTIVES & SKILLS: After you read this chapter, you will be able to:

Introduction to Outlook and Email

OBJECTIVE 1: IDENTIFY THE COMPONENTS OF THE OUTLOOK WINDOW 4
Start Outlook

OBJECTIVE 2: MANAGE EMAIL 9
Send a Message, Read a Message, Reply to a Message, Attach a File, Open an Attachment, Create a New Folder, Store a Message in the Folder, Add a Signature to a Mail Message, Flag a Message for Follow Up, Manage the Mailbox

HANDS-ON EXERCISE 1:
Introduction to Outlook and Email 20

Outlook Contacts

OBJECTIVE 3: MANAGE CONTACTS 30
Create a Contact List, Add a Contact Category, Change the Contacts View, Organize Contacts

Create a Contact Group, Use the Contact Group to Send Email, Print Contacts as a PDF File

HANDS-ON EXERCISE 2:
Outlook Contacts 35

Outlook Calendar, Task List, and Notes

OBJECTIVE 4: MANAGE THE OUTLOOK CALENDAR 42
Enter an Appointment, Add Conditional Formatting, Share a Calendar, Print a Calendar as a PDF File

OBJECTIVE 5: MANAGE TASKS AND NOTES 45
Create a Task, Print a Task List as a PDF File, Create a Note, Print a Note as a PDF File

HANDS-ON EXERCISE 3:
Outlook Calendar, Task List, and Notes 48

CASE STUDY | T-Shirts to Go

Mary Taylor and Jake Edwards are friends of yours. You recently worked together on an entrepreneurship project in your business class and came away with big plans. The dream is to participate in the Entrepreneurship National Championship held in June. The team has already designed a logo and now wants to make and sell silk-screened T-shirts to raise money to attend the weeklong event. You are all very busy running the fledgling operation, and have organization, scheduling, and communications needs with which Outlook can help. You need to send messages to teammates, distributors, and suppliers. You must be able to attach drawings, worksheets, and documents to the messages.

Members of your team also want to set up meetings. Given your busy schedules, you want to print calendars to post on the team's message board, and you would like reminders to popup onscreen when it is time to go to an appointment. The team needs to keep a list of things to be done and would like to do this electronically.

You will need the names of all suppliers that you use, including T-shirt distributors, fabric paint suppliers, ground shipping companies, and student workers. The team plans to store the email address, phone number, cell phone number, mailing address, and other pertinent information for each of their contacts. You need an efficient way to keep the contact information organized. You would also like to note whether a contact is a supplier, a student, an alumnus, or belongs to some other category.

Finally, team members have, on occasion, forgotten what files they used or in what folder they saved them. They would like to be able to locate recently used files easily.

Managing Email, Contacts, Tasks, and Calendars

CHAPTER 1

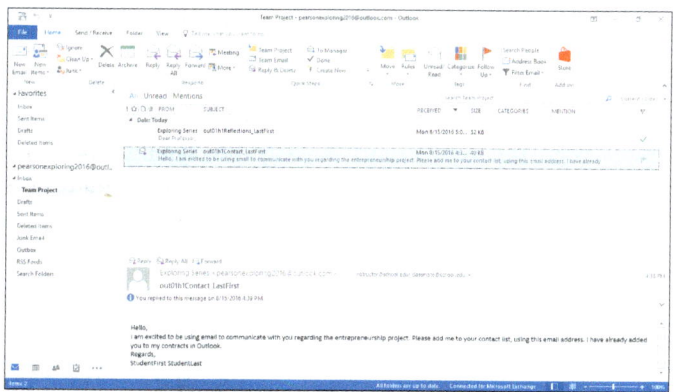
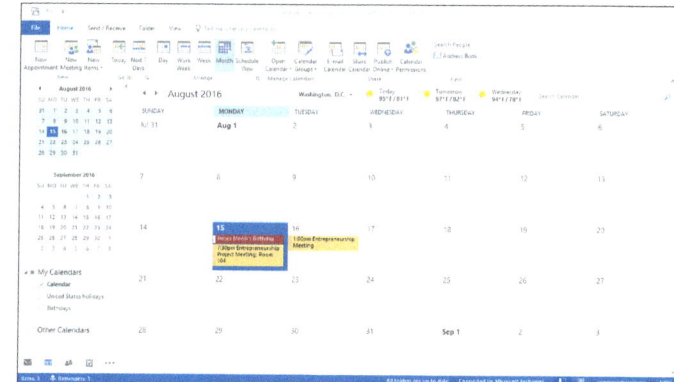
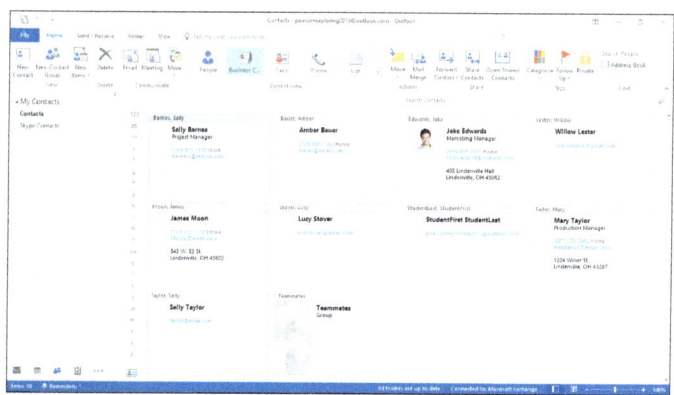
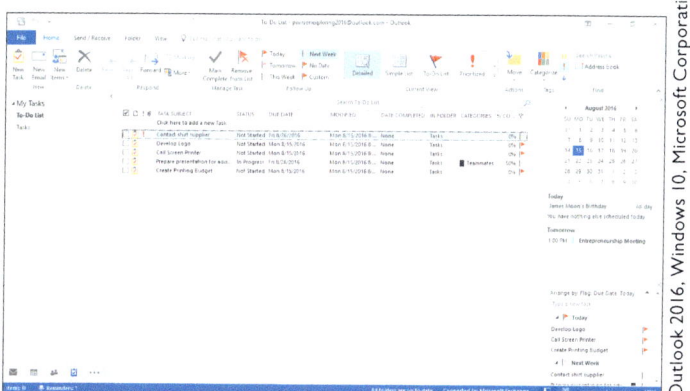

FIGURE 1.1 T-Shirts to Go Documents

CASE STUDY | T-Shirts to Go

Starting Files	Email and Files to be Submitted
out01h1Ideas	out01h1Contact_LastFirst
out01h1Logo	RE:out01h1Contact_LastFirst
out01h2ContactPhoto	out01h1Attachment_LastFirst
	out01h1Reflections_LastFirst
	out01h1TeamFolder_LastFirst.png
	out01h2Contacts_LastFirst
	out01h2TeammatesContacts_LastFirst.pdf
	out01h3Calendar_LastFirst
	out01h3Tasks_LastFirst.pdf
	out01h3Note_LastFirst.pdf

Managing Email, Contacts, Tasks, and Calendars • Outlook   3

Introduction to Outlook and Email

Outlook is an integral part of Microsoft Office 2016. It can be used on a stand-alone PC to manage your own work or on a network to facilitate communication with others in your organization. You can even access Outlook.com on your mobile device. Think of Outlook as a personal assistant or desktop manager that keeps track of all types of information for you. Intuitively, you already know how Outlook works. Do you carry an address book or an appointment book? Do you write yourself a list of things to do? Do you send the same message to a number of people? Outlook automates these processes, and in so doing adds considerable flexibility to the way you enter and refer to your data.

The Outlook application installed on your local computer enables you to complete a variety of tasks. It is installed as you install Office 2016. You can also sign in to Outlook.com using your Microsoft account, and perform the same tasks using the Internet interface. The Outlook.com account can sync to your Outlook desktop client and keep you up to date. This chapter focuses on using the desktop Outlook application, but the components and tools are similar in Outlook.com, as shown in Figure 1.2.

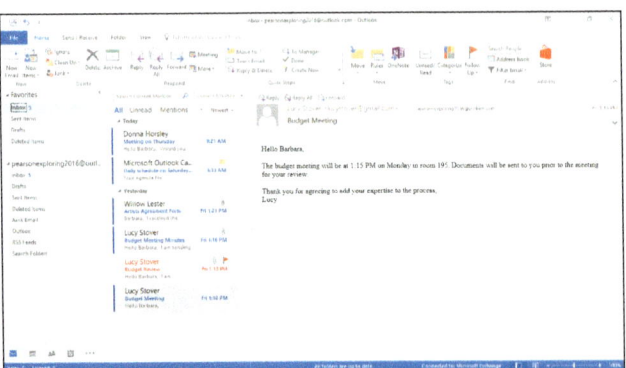 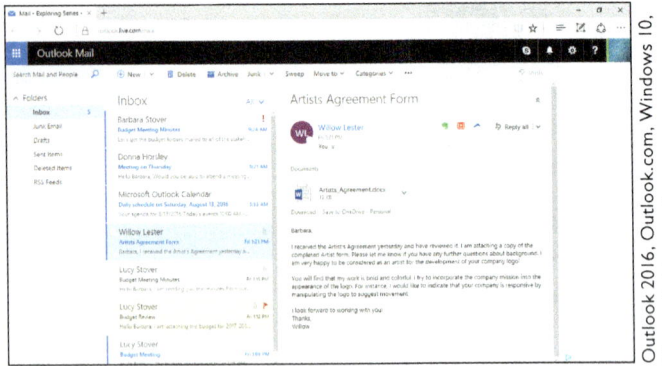

FIGURE 1.2 Outlook Desktop Client and Outlook.com

> **TIP: WORKING WITH OTHER EMAIL ACCOUNTS**
> You can add other email accounts, such as Gmail, to your Outlook client. This enables you to see email from all of your accounts when you work in Outlook. Use Backstage view to set up additional accounts.

In this section, you will learn how to use Outlook with a brief overview of each component: Mail, Calendar, Tasks, and Contacts. You will move immediately to email, perhaps the most widely used component in Outlook. You will explore or review the basic commands present in any email system to compose, send, read, and reply to email messages. You will attach files to an email message and create different folders to organize the messages you send and receive.

Identifying the Components of the Outlook Window

Outlook 2016 contains a Ribbon to give you access to commands, along with panes to display information. The Ribbon and panes change based on the Outlook component you are using. When you open Outlook, the email component displays, as shown in Figure 1.3. Depending on the component you select, the central portion of the screen will change.

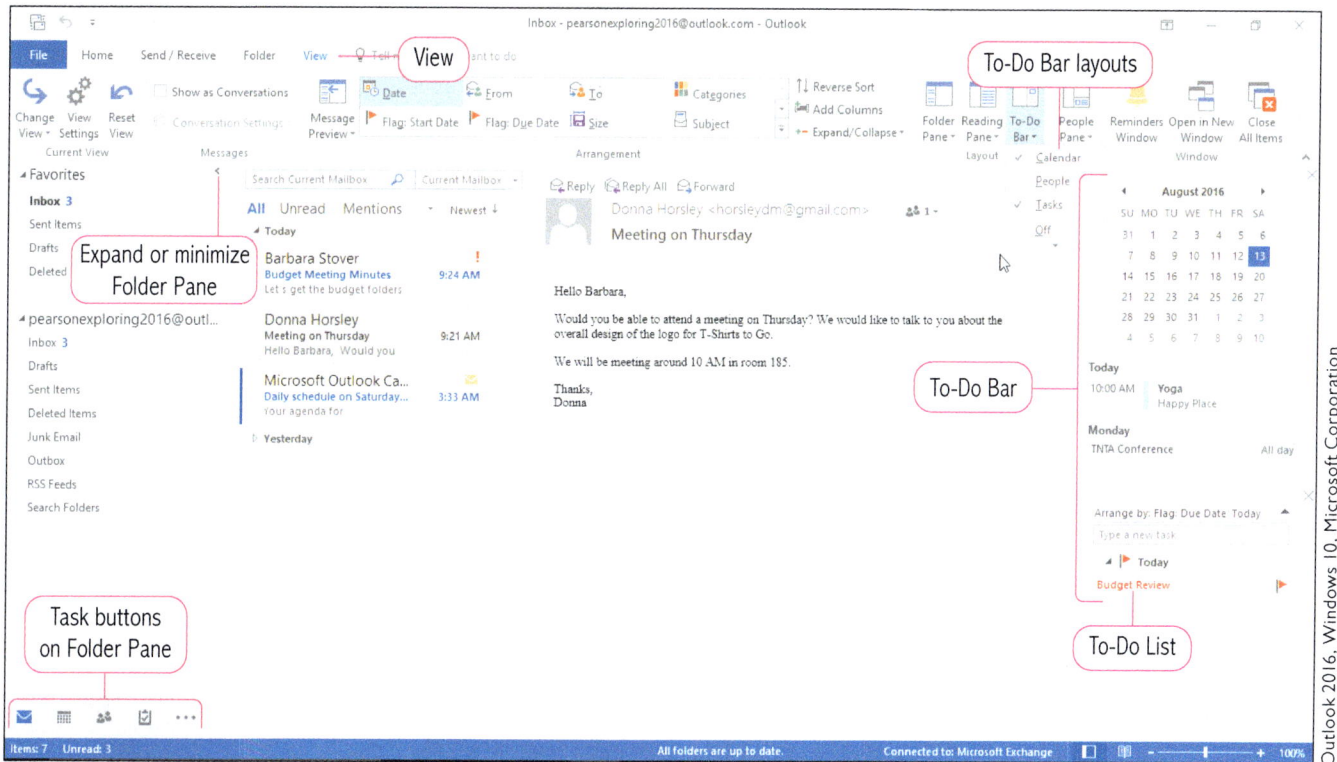

FIGURE 1.3 Outlook Window Displaying Mail Component

The **Folder Pane** contains folders, calendars, or categories for organizing information for each of the components of Outlook. The task buttons at the bottom of the Folder Pane enable you to switch to the component you want to use. Similar to all panes in Outlook, clicking the arrow at the top of the pane toggles the pane opened or closed. In a window where you have reduced the size of the window, you can pin the Folder Pane so it remains full size. If you close a pane in Outlook that you would later like to use, click the View tab and select a layout option from the Layout group, as shown in Figure 1.3, on the submenu to restore the layout.

To get a quick glance at a component that is not active, point to the task button on the Folder Pane. Your schedule, favorite contacts, and tasks will display in small thumbnails, providing you with brief information without completely opening that component.

> **TIP: CHANGING THE TASK BUTTON ORDER**
> If you would like to change the order of the task buttons on the bottom of the Folder Pane, click the [...] button and select Navigation Options. Select the task button you want to move, and click Move Up or Move Down as needed. You can also just drag the buttons into the location you want.

View Mail

The Mail component, shown in Figure 1.4, displays Favorites and Personal Folders for organizing email messages. These folders are created automatically when Outlook is installed. The **Inbox** is the default folder for receiving email. The name of the person sending the email, the subject, and time the message was received are listed for each message. You can change the preview, selecting different display options for the message, using the Message Preview command on the View tab. A paperclip icon indicates messages that have attachments, files that have been added to the message. Additional icons enable you to flag the message and assign categories. The messages are shown in the order in which they are received, although you can sort them in different ways, if desired. The **Reading Pane**, shown to the right of the Inbox in Figure 1.4, displays the text of the selected message. The Reading Pane can be positioned on the right, on the bottom, or turned off altogether. The People icon, displayed in the message header, provides information about alternative methods for contacting the person. When you have a photograph associated with the contact, the picture will display in the header.

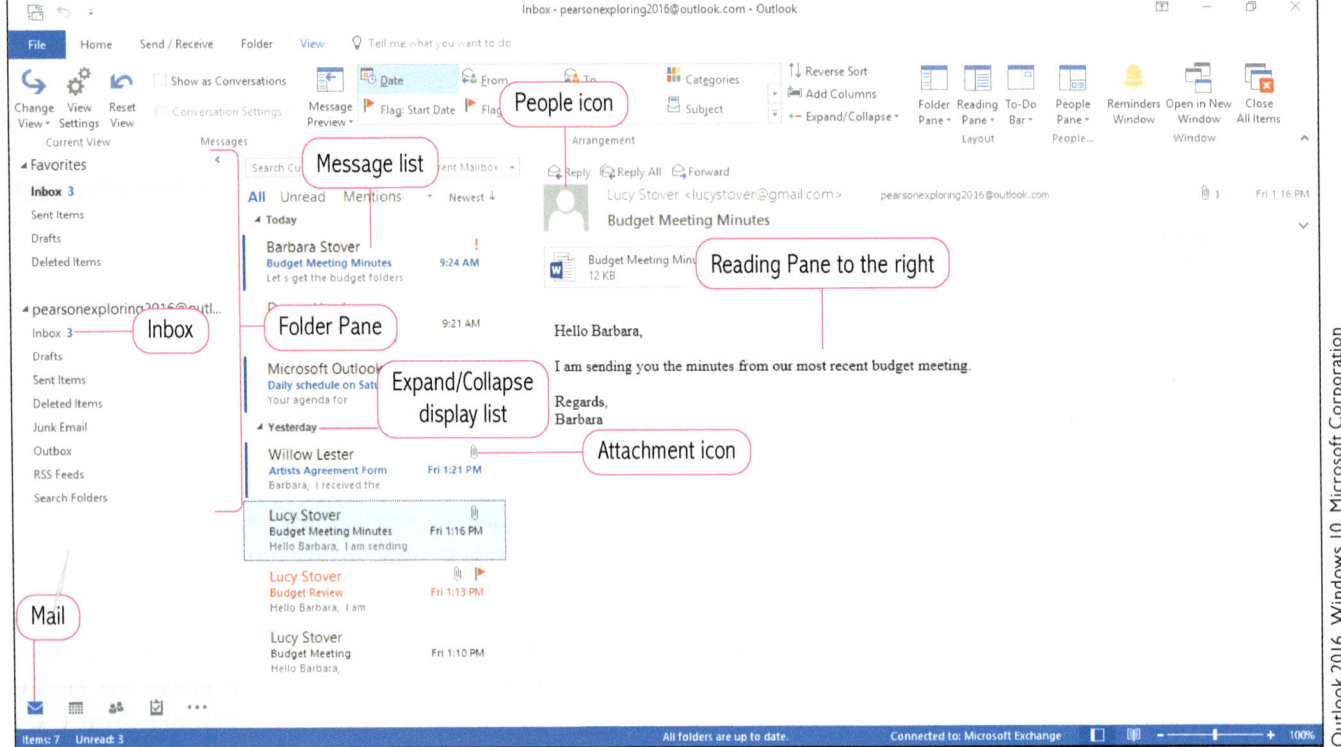

FIGURE 1.4 Outlook Mail Component

TIP: IT IS SYNERGISTIC

The components in Outlook are thoroughly integrated with one another, making each function more valuable as a part of the whole. For example, you can automatically notify others of meetings by sending an email from the Calendar or from entries in Contacts. You can also go in the other direction and create entries in your Contacts list or events on your calendar directly from an email message.

View Appointments with the Calendar

The Calendar component (see Figure 1.5) gives access to personal and professional calendars. When the Calendar component is selected, a calendar and a task list are displayed in the window. The calendar can be shown by day, week, or month. You can create a detailed appointment book using the Calendar. Outlook calendar items can be set to remind you of upcoming appointments. You can create recurring appointments, such as inputting your class schedule and scheduling all of your Monday CIS150 classes with one entry. You can print, email, share, and publish your calendar.

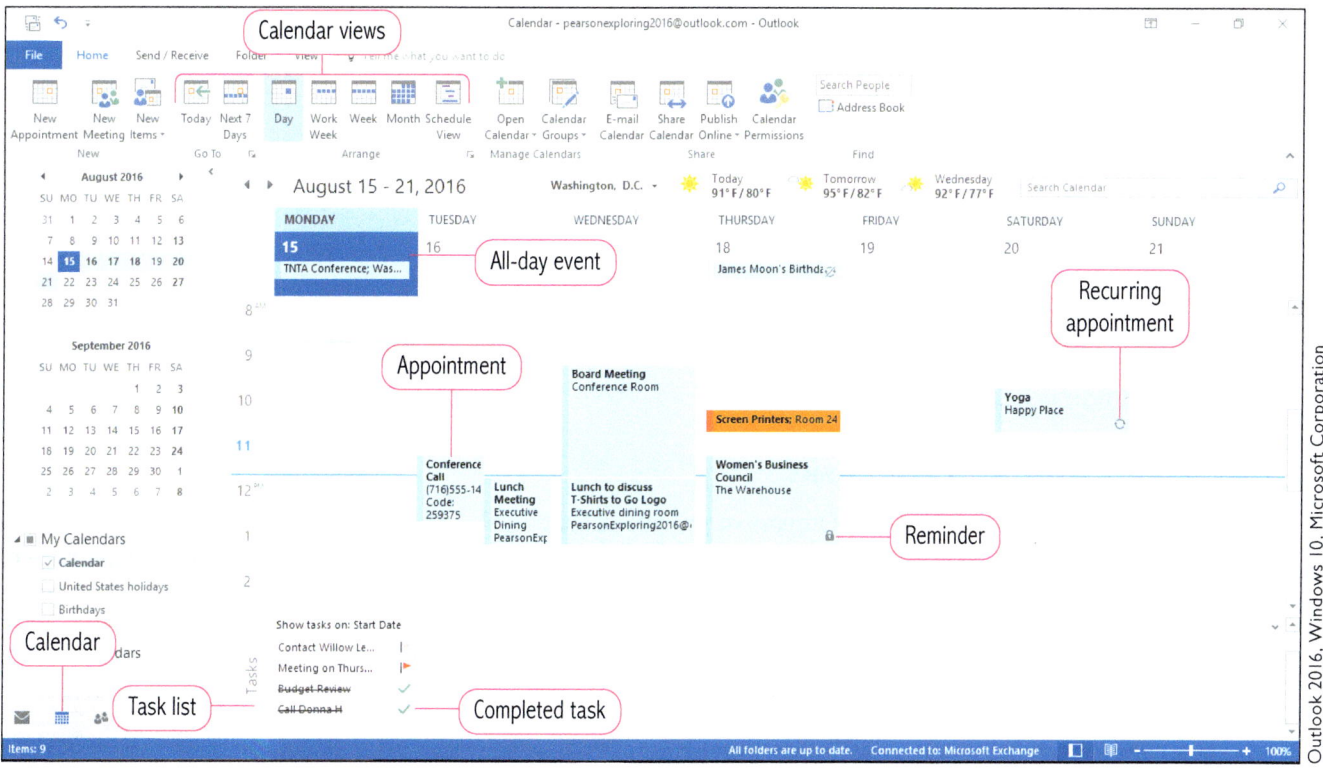

FIGURE 1.5 Outlook Calendar Component

View Contacts

The Contacts (or People) component (see Figure 1.6) provides detailed information about your contacts and is often referred to as the address book. Options for different views of the information and searches make it easy to find your contacts. You can enter as much (or as little) information for each contact as you like. Photographs of the people can be added to the contact information to enable you to identify the contact quickly. You can display the contacts as a list, business cards, cards, or as a phone list. You may assign categories to the contacts and view them by category. Even better is the ability to use the information across the Microsoft Office 2016 applications. For example, when using Word, you can access addresses from your Outlook Contacts to address a letter. You can also print the Contacts folder as a backup of the information and sync with the Contacts list in Outlook.com so they are always available to you.

Introduction to Outlook and Email • Outlook

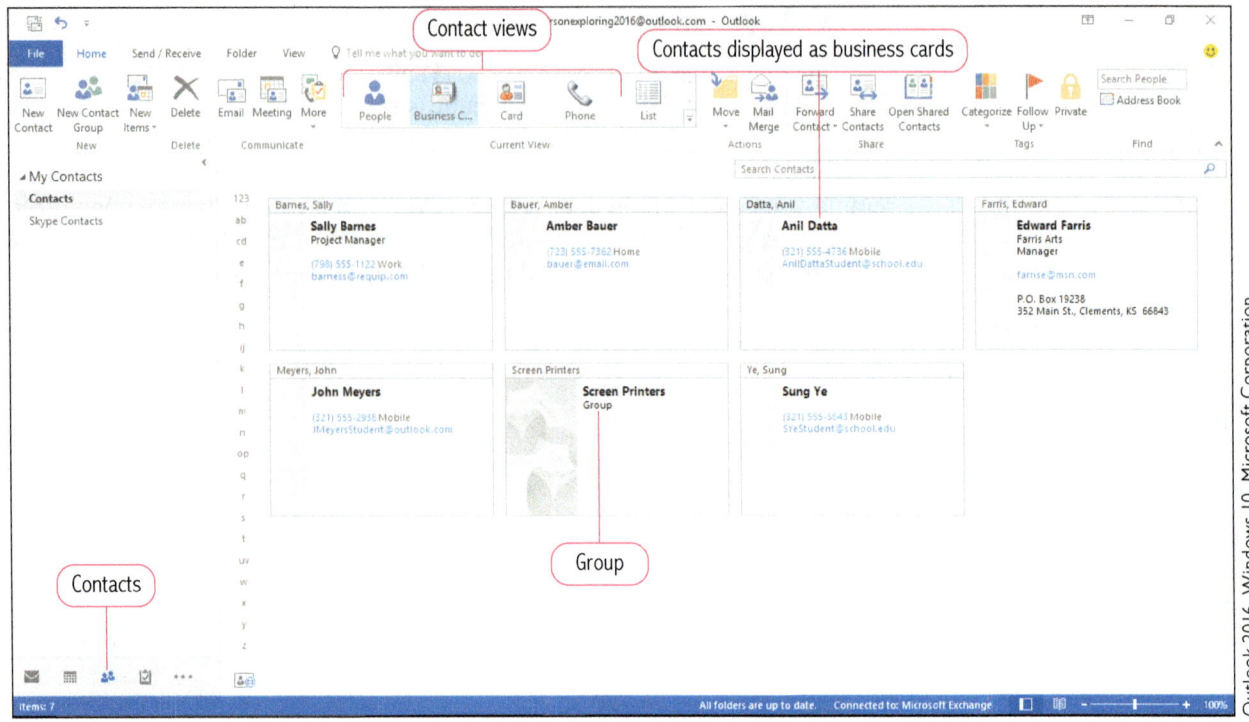

FIGURE 1.6 Outlook Contacts Component

View Tasks

The Tasks component provides a list of tasks. The Folder Pane contains a To-Do List and a Tasks list. The To-Do List is derived from both the tasks you set and any follow-up tags that you set while working in the Mail component. The **To-Do Bar** provides an overview of the calendar, upcoming appointments, and tasks. Open the To-Do Bar in any Outlook component using the To-Do Bar command in the Layout group on the View tab. The To-Do bar, with a calendar and task list, is shown in Figure 1.7.

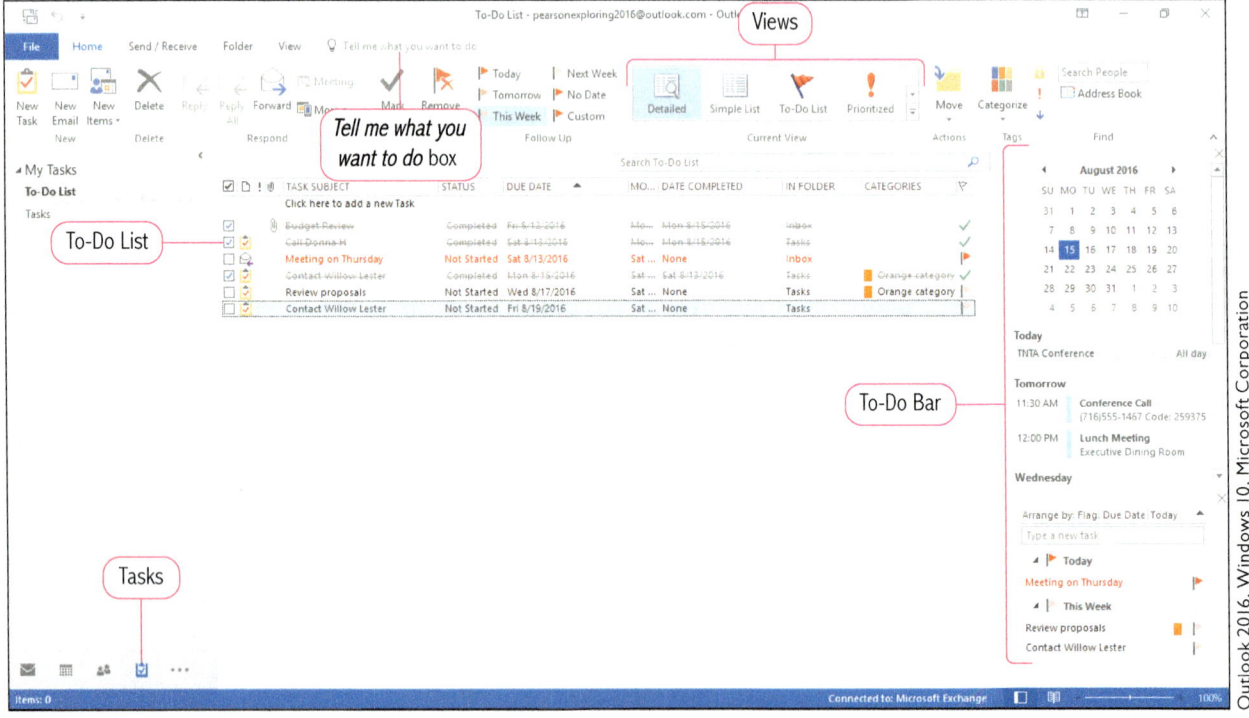

FIGURE 1.7 Outlook Tasks Component

CHAPTER 1 • Managing Email, Contacts, Tasks, and Calendars

When the Tasks component is in use, the work area shows a listing of all of the tasks. You may change the view, displaying the tasks in a number of different ways, including by due date or by importance. You may also assign different categories to the tasks and view them by category. When creating a task, you specify a subject, start and due dates, status, priorities, and reminders. You cannot specify times and locations with tasks, as you can with Calendar appointments. You may also add tasks while using the Calendar component by typing them on the day they are due on the Tasks list at the bottom of the calendar (refer to Figure 1.5). When you complete a task, a quick click marks it as completed on the task list. The To-Do List can be printed for viewing when you are not at your computer.

> **TIP: TASKS SYNCHRONIZATION**
> Outlook.com email accounts set up in Outlook 2016 will sync to Outlook.com in the cloud.

Get Help with Outlook

In Outlook, as with all Office applications, help is readily available to assist you in understanding the components. Click in the *Tell me what you want to do* box at the top of the Ribbon (refer to Figure 1.7) and begin to type your question. Outlook will offer you options, such as *Get help on* or *Smart Lookup on*, and further try to anticipate what you want to do and assist you in doing it. Smart Lookup uses a Bing.com search to provide answers from the Web and a definition if you typed a term. Using the *Tell me what you want to do* box is another way to get to different components of Outlook. For instance, type Calendar in the box, and the calendar will display on the screen.

Managing Email

Electronic mail, or email, although conceptually the same as writing a letter and sending it through the U.S. Postal Service, has one very significant advantage—email messages are delivered almost instantly anywhere in the world via the Internet. All email systems work essentially the same way. A **mail client**, a program such as Microsoft Outlook 2016 on your computer or a web-based application such as Outlook.com, enables you to compose, send, and receive email messages. Outlook, as your mail client, sets up the connection with the mail server to receive your incoming messages and to deliver the messages you send.

A **mail server** is a special-purpose computer with an Internet connection such as you might have in your campus computer network, or it is a computer at your Internet Service Provider such as Verizon, Comcast, or your cable company. The mail server functions as a central post office and provides private mailboxes to people authorized to use its services. The mail server receives messages around the clock from the Internet and any local networks that are attached to it, and then stores messages for you until you log in to retrieve them.

In order to use Outlook to connect to a mail server, you must have already established an email account and it must be set up within Outlook. The many methods for doing so are beyond the scope of this text. You should check with your instructor or campus help desk for information on how to connect to your campus mail server or your Internet Service Provider (ISP) technical support if you have an email account through another service.

> **TIP: EMAIL PROTOCOLS**
> The email protocol that you use will affect some of the features available in Outlook. If you use an Exchange server or a Post Office Protocol (POP3), you will have full access to the features. If you use an Internet Access Message Protocol (IMAP)—for instance, in a Gmail or Yahoo Mail account—you will notice that some features are limited or not available. This book was written using an Exchange server account.

When you open Outlook, it connects you to the server, where you gain access to your mailbox via a username and a password. Your username is a unique word that identifies you to the server; your password works in combination with your username to protect your account from unauthorized use by others.

> **TIP: SECURE PASSWORDS**
> Passwords should be selected carefully and not shared with other people. Select a password with a mix of upper- and lowercase letters, symbols, punctuation, and numbers for added security. Microsoft suggests a password should be at least 8 characters and can be up to 15 characters. Avoid using an easy-to-guess password, such as your pet's name. It should be something that you can remember. A good password might be the first letters of each of the words of a favorite quotation with numbers and punctuation substituting for some of the characters. For example, if your favorite quotation is "You can lead a horse to water, but you can't make him drink," then your password could be "yclah2w!Bycmhd."

You can view and reply to messages when not connected to the Internet, but you will not receive or send messages without an Internet connection. Once you log in to the mail server, outgoing mail is uploaded from your computer to the server, where it is sent on its way across a local area network to another person within your organization or across the Internet to recipients wherever they are located. New mail is downloaded from the server and stored in the Inbox in Outlook on your computer.

Manage the Inbox

Figure 1.8 displays another view of the Inbox as it appears in Outlook. The Folder Pane still displays the folder list, but in this view, the Reading Pane is at the bottom of the window. The message list at the top of the window lists each incoming message, the name of the sender, the subject, the date and time the message was received, and the size of the message. You can also see the first words of the message as a preview. In this view, the most recent messages appear at the top of the list. Look carefully at the messages in the Inbox and note the formatting that indicates message status and contents.

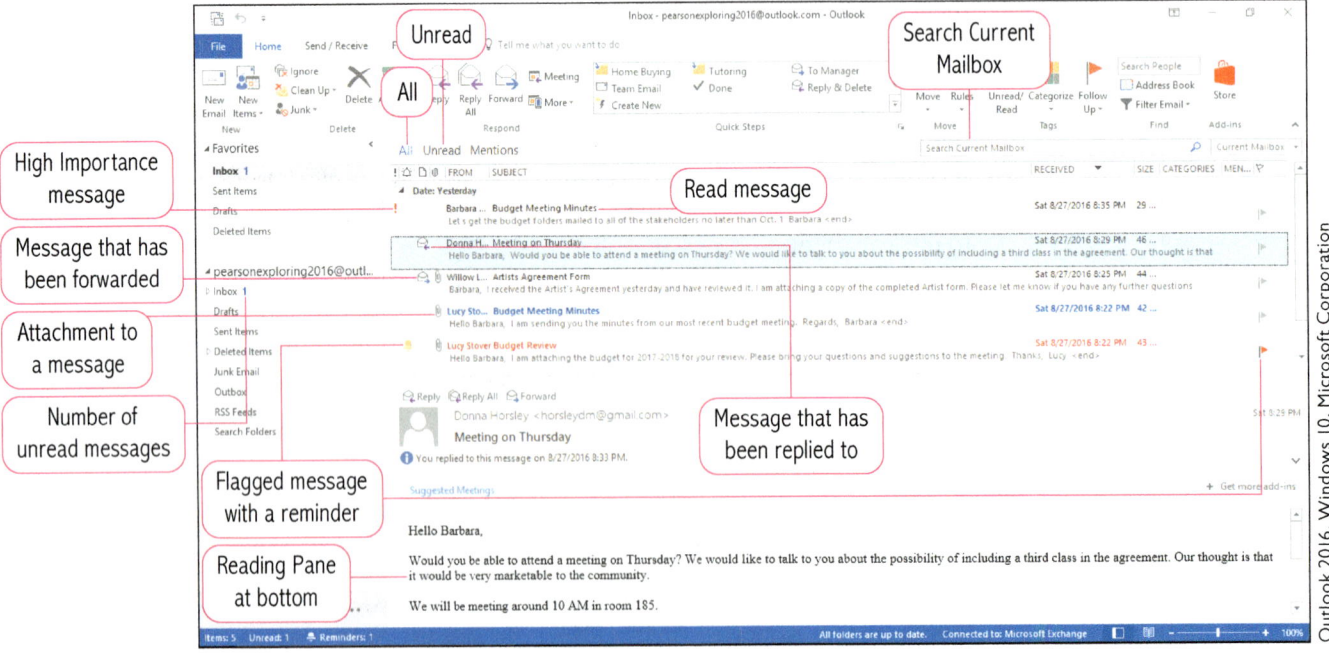

FIGURE 1.8 Inbox View

CHAPTER 1 • Managing Email, Contacts, Tasks, and Calendars

> **TIP: MESSAGE LIST COMMANDS**
> Next to each message in the message list are icons that enable you to manage the messages. Point to a message and click the flag to set up a follow-up reminder. Click the X to move the message to the Deleted Items folder.

The number next to the folders in the Folder Pane shows a count of unread messages. Messages that have been read appear in regular type on the message list; messages that have not been read appear in boldface. An exclamation point next to the message indicates that the sender marked the message as being of high importance. The recipient of a message can flag it for follow up, designated with a flag icon in the message list. The icon with a left-pointing arrow denotes a message that has been replied to. The message icon with a right-pointing arrow indicates that the message has been forwarded to another recipient. Messages with attachments show a paperclip icon. If you are using an Exchange server or POP3, you can flag messages with a reminder that displays an alarm icon (bell) in the message list.

You can display all of the messages, or just the unread messages, by clicking the All or Unread button at the top of the message list (refer to Figure 1.8). The message list can be sorted in a wide variety of ways, including by date, who the message is from, subject, and attachments. Messages in the message list can be filtered to display only messages that meet a criterion. Click Filter Email in the Find Group on the Home tab and select the filter to apply. The choices include Unread, Has Attachments, This Week (with date settings), Categorized, Flagged, Important, and Sent To: Me or CC: Me. You can create a custom filter by using More Filters, which works like a search, where you type the search criterion to filter the message list to items that match the criterion.

A Search Current Mailbox box at the top of the message list enables you to search for email that contains the phrase you type in the box. For instance, you remember an email from Mary that discussed the colors of T-shirts she could provide. You can type *Mary* and *color* in the Instant Search box to see any email that contains these words.

Messages can be grouped into conversations. **Conversations** are groups of messages that share the same subject line. To group messages into conversations, check the box next to Show as Conversations on the View tab and select *This folder* or *All mailboxes* to display as a conversation. Small, open arrows next to the envelope icon that display when you have selected the Show as Conversations checkbox, indicate that the conversation can be expanded to show the correspondence related to that message, as shown in Figure 1.9. With the conversation expanded, the original subject that started the conversation is shown as a header at the top of the conversation group, with the related correspondence below including replies you may have sent. As the conversation continues, the newest messages appear below the subject header in the conversation group. When a new message arrives, the conversation group moves to the top of your Inbox message list to alert you that new activity is occurring in the conversation. The subject line of unread messages appears in a bold font. Further small dots and lines indicate the relationship of the messages. The expanded conversation is collapsed by clicking the arrow to the left of the conversation message header.

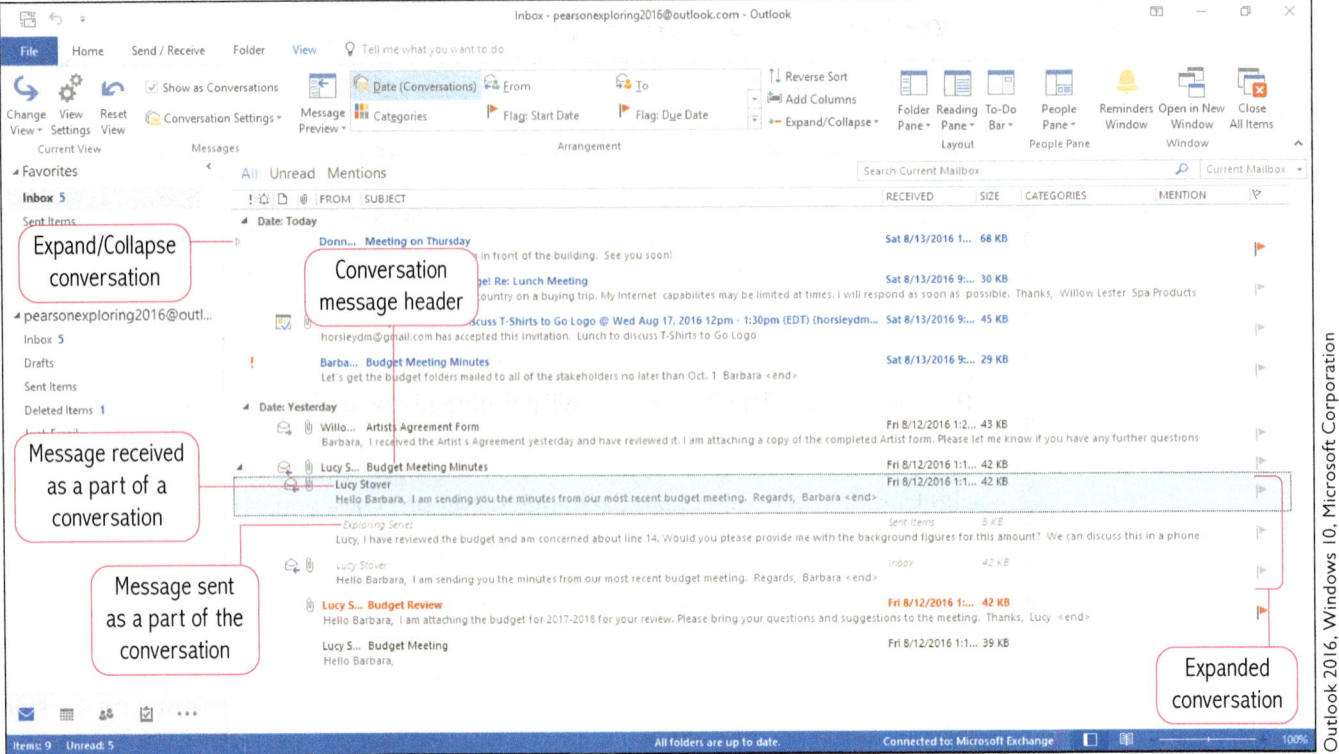

FIGURE 1.9 Inbox Conversation Expanded

Conversations can be categorized, flagged, cleaned up, ignored, or deleted. You can categorize messages and conversations with blocks of color so that they are readily recognizable. You can flag them for follow up. Conversations or messages within the conversation can be deleted. In addition, you can use Clean Up Conversation in the Delete group. Outlook determines if a message is completely contained in another message (such as might occur if you reply to a message), considers that message redundant, and moves it to the **Deleted Items folder**, which is a recycle bin that contains messages you have deleted. Ignored conversations and all future redundant messages in that conversation are automatically moved to the Deleted Items folder. Commands to complete these actions are available on the Home tab. Select the conversation header and apply the desired actions.

> **TIP: NOT AS PRIVATE AS YOU THINK**
> One of the most significant differences between email and regular mail is privacy—or the lack thereof. When you receive a sealed letter through the mail, you can assume that no one else has read the letter. Not so with email. Email messages are easily forwarded and passed on to others without your knowledge. The network administrator can read the messages in your inbox, and indeed, many employers regularly monitor employees' email. Do not assume that deleting a message protects your privacy, because most organizations maintain extensive backup systems and can recover a deleted message. In other words, never put anything in an email message that you would be uncomfortable seeing in tomorrow's newspaper.

Create an Email Message

STEP 1 Creating an email message is easy. Just click New Email in the New group on the Home tab of the Mail component to display a window similar to Figure 1.10. Notice that the Ribbon contains various tabs and commands specific to composing email messages. The

12 CHAPTER 1 • Managing Email, Contacts, Tasks, and Calendars

Message tab contains most message composition functions, and the Insert tab enables you to make additions to your message, such as pictures, signatures, business cards, and more. The Options tab is for special services such as requesting a Read Receipt, and the Format Text tab is for manipulating the message text. The Review tab enables you to check the spelling and grammar of the message, along with other review options.

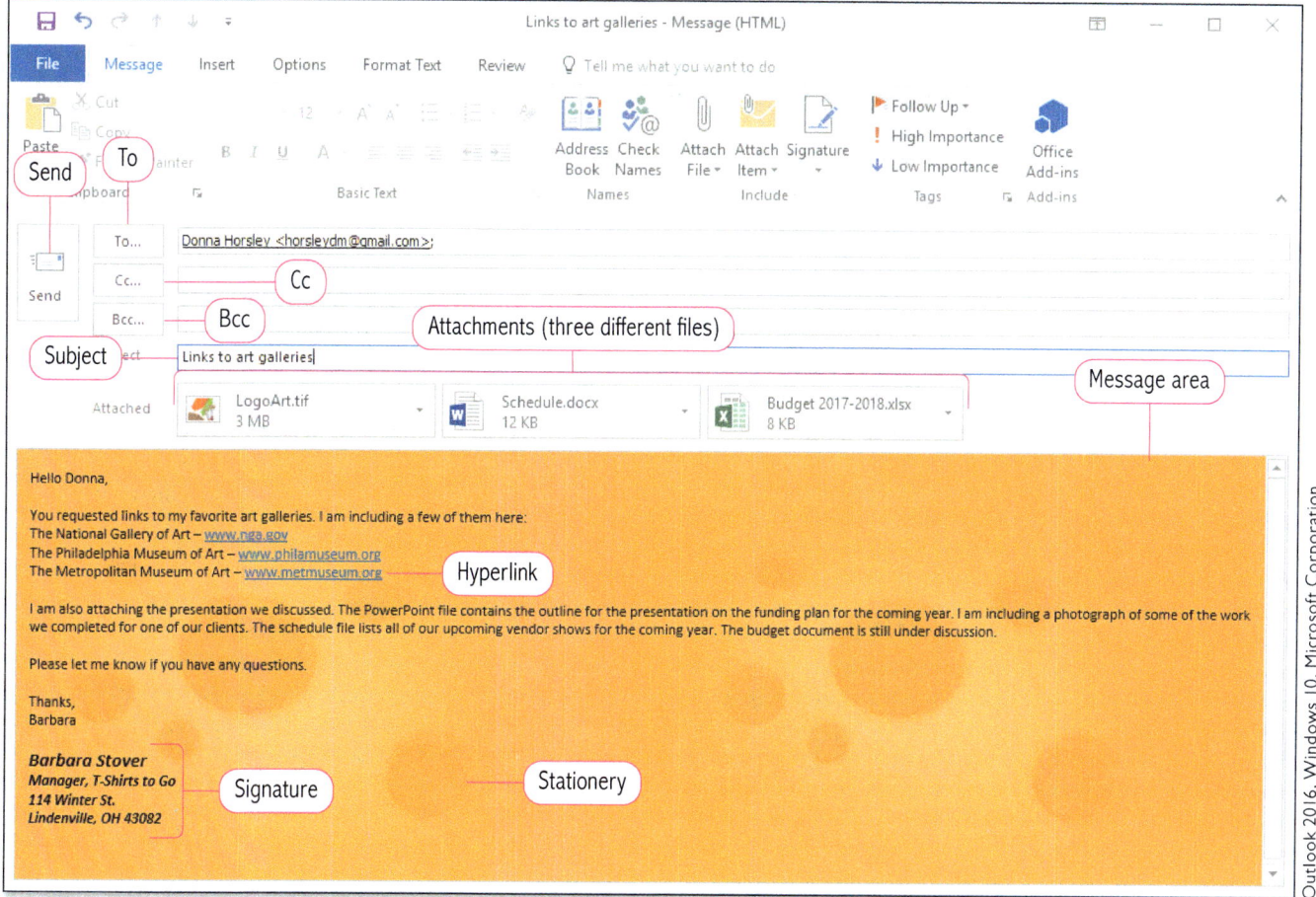

FIGURE 1.10 Compose a Message

Select the Recipients for Your Message

The functions of the various text boxes at the top of the message window are apparent from their names (refer to Figure 1.10). The To box, for example, is for the email address of the recipient(s). The Cc box (courtesy or carbon copy) is used to send copies of the message to other people. The blind carbon copy (Bcc) box is used to send blind copies of the email to someone, meaning that the other recipients of the message do not know that this person received a copy. A Bcc works well if you are sending a message to a large number of people and you do not want to reveal their email addresses. Simply use your own email address in the To box and place all of the other recipient email addresses in the Bcc box. By default, the Bcc box does not appear automatically. Click the Options tab, and select Bcc from the Show Fields group. After you complete this action, the Bcc field appears each time you begin a new message.

> **TIP: BLIND CARBON COPIES**
> In business, blind carbon copies are useful. If you send a newsletter to all of your customers, for instance, you should preserve the privacy of the recipients by not listing their email addresses. This also keeps them from receiving email that is sent through the Reply All function. Another reason for using blind carbon copy in the business environment is to document an email message by sending it to someone else, such as your supervisor. It is very effective to write a positive note to a fellow employee for a job well done, and to blind carbon copy the person's supervisor.

> **TIP: TO Cc OR NOT TO Cc**
> Think carefully before you indicate that a copy should be sent to someone. Do they really need to see the message? Do they want their email address revealed to the other recipients? Avoid filling mailboxes of your friends, family, and business associates with unnecessary mail. They will appreciate your courtesy.

The Subject box is filled in with an appropriate indicator of the message contents so that the recipient can determine at a glance what the message is about. Consider subject lines that clearly indicate the purpose of the message, such as "Appointment request to discuss logo." If you have a question about something, include the word *question*. For example, "Marketing Plan Budget Question" would signal the recipient that you want additional information about the budget. Instructors often request specific subject lines for assignments so they can quickly identify the contents of email and file it in appropriate folders.

Compose the Message

Enter the text of the message in the message area below the subject line, and click Send to mail it. The message itself can be simple or more sophisticated, and you can use stationery to create an interesting background, and include hyperlinks, attachments, and a signature, as shown in the example in Figure 1.10. Outlook documents are Web-enabled, meaning that you or the recipient can click a hyperlink within an email message, and provided you have an Internet connection, be automatically connected to the webpage.

> **TIP: ADDING A MENTION TO A MESSAGE**
> To add special emphasis to a person's name in your email message and automatically add them to the recipient list, type @ in front of the person's name. As you start to type the name, Outlook will offer suggestions based on your contacts list. Select the correct person and the full name will appear in the message. You can modify the mention to display only their first or last name. To see messages in which you are mentioned, click Mentions above the message list in the Mail component window.

The message in Figure 1.10 shows Outlook stationery that you can select as a background for your messages, and a signature. You can add stationery or themes to your messages to dress them up or to give them an individualized appearance that your recipients will recognize as yours. Outlook handles stationery as it does themes. Select the stationery you want to use from the Options page in Backstage view. The stationery theme supplies a background color or image and formats the fonts. Additional themes and stationery are available on Microsoft Office Online. The stationery or theme will be applied to all messages you create until you change it.

As you create email, whether as a reply or as a newly composed message, it is worthwhile to keep netiquette in mind. **Netiquette** is etiquette for the Internet, and is a group of commonly accepted good manners. Formal messages, that you might create for job searches or conversations with professors or clients, especially require the use of netiquette. Netiquette guidelines are shown in Table 1.1.

TABLE 1.1 Netiquette Guidelines

Netiquette	Guideline
Appropriate Language	Avoid abbreviations, slang, and Instant Message shortcuts. Write complete sentences with proper grammar and punctuation. Use sentence case. Avoid all capital letters, as they indicate shouting. Proofread and check the spelling of your work.
Subject Line	Indicate the contents of the message. Only mark a message as high importance if it truly is.
Content	Begin the message with a salutation. End it with a closing. State your message concisely. Indicate the expected outcome or recipient response to your message. If a time frame is appropriate to your expectation, be sure to state it clearly. Avoid composing messages while angry. Remember that email is not private. Avoid saying anything that you would not be willing to see on the front page of the newspaper.
Attachments	Limit the size of files that you attach to the email message. Make sure the recipient has the software to open the attachments on his or her local computer; otherwise, consider saving in a universal format, such as PDF. Note that some company email servers block certain types of files, such as .zip or image files, because they may contain viruses.
Forwarding Messages	Before you send something out to everyone on your distribution list, consider whether it has worth to everyone. Avoid chain letter forwarding. Avoid sending jokes unless you are absolutely sure that the recipient will appreciate the humor.
Responding to Messages	Respond to messages quickly. If you cannot complete a detailed response, let the sender know and flag the message for follow up. It may be easier to add your comments directly into the original email as your response. In that case, indicate that your replies are incorporated in the original message, and note how you are distinguishing your responses (i.e. by font color or highlights).

Reply to or Forward an Email Message

STEP 2 Replying to an existing message is similar in concept to creating a new message, except that Outlook automatically enters the addressee for you. While viewing the message to which you want to respond, click Reply, and then enter the text of your message. If needed, you can enter additional recipients. The Subject line contains the subject from the original message, with RE: added to the beginning. You can change the subject by adding to or typing over it.

The Reply All option will route the message to the sender of the message along with any other recipients included in the message, except those copied as Bcc in the original message. The Forward option takes the original message and sends it to the people you specify. It also adds FW: to the Subject line to notify the people that this is a forwarded message. In the business environment, it is a good idea to check with the sender of the message before forwarding it to someone else.

> **To reply to a message, complete the following steps:**
> 1. Select the message and click Reply, Reply All, or Forward in the Respond group.
> 2. Enter the recipient's email address in the To box (for forwarded messages), or review the automatically entered email address (when using Reply or Reply All).
> 3. Note that the subject is entered automatically from the originating email. You can add to or edit the text of the original message, or you can add your text above the line that separates the forwarded portion from the new message.
> 4. Click Send when you finish, and the message will be on its way to the new recipient(s).

Attach Files

STEP 3 >> An ***attached file*** is a file created in another software application and then appended to the email message for transmission to the recipient. The message in Figure 1.10 contains three attached files—a picture file, a Word document, and an Excel workbook. The recipient has the ability to view, save, and/or edit the attached file on his or her computer in its original format. The recipient double-clicks the attachment link to edit the attachment file. The attachment opens in the appropriate software for the type of file. The file is edited using the application in which it was originally created. To save the file directly to the local computer without first viewing it, right-click the attachment link and click Save As.

You can attach any file from your computer to an email message, but the recipient must have the related application in order to open and edit the file. Click Attach file in the Include group on the Message tab and navigate to the location of the file. Select the file and click Insert.

As an alternative, you can drag the file from File Explorer onto the message to attach it. You may notice that large files sometimes take time to send, depending on the speed of your Internet connection. If you have large files or multiple files to send, it is a good practice to zip them before attaching them to email messages.

When you receive an email message with an attachment, you can preview the attachment contents in the Reading Pane, but cannot make changes to the attachment itself. You will need to open the file with the appropriate application in order to make changes. Through the commands on the Attachments tab, which displays when you select the attachment in the message, you can print, save, remove, or copy the attachment.

> **TIP: PRINT AN EMAIL MESSAGE**
> You can print email messages by clicking the File tab and clicking Print to display the Print choice and preview. The Memo Style prints the selected message along with the header information of whom the message is from, when it was sent, to whom it was sent, and the subject. The Table Style prints a listing similar to the message list with all of the messages, the header information, and a line from the message. The Preview pane displays the message as it will look when printed. Also, use the Print Options dialog box to select the printer, the number of copies, and the page range. Click Print to begin printing the message.

Add a Signature

STEP 4 >> An email signature contains your relevant information, such as name, address, company name and logo, and phone number. In business, it is best to include your title and contact information with each message you send. During a job search, your signature might include your college, anticipated degree, and permanent address. You append signatures to messages you send or set Outlook to end your email messages automatically with a signature. This will save you time and relieve you of having to type your name, title, address, telephone, and other information at the end of each message.

To create a signature, complete the following steps:

1. Click the File tab, click the Options in the left pane, and then click Mail in the left pane.
2. Click Signatures in the Compose messages section (just below Spelling and Autocorrect) to display the Signatures and Stationery dialog box.
3. Click New, type a name for the signature, and then click OK.
4. Click in the Edit Signature box, and type the information for the signature. You can modify the font or add a picture (such as your company logo) to add interest to your signature.
5. Click OK to close the Create Signature dialog box, and click OK to close the Outlook Options dialog box. To test the signature, click New Email to create a new message. Your signature will automatically appear in the message area.

You can set up additional signatures for a variety of purposes and choose from them by clicking Signature in the Include group on the Message tab or Insert tab in the message window.

Manage Mail Folders

STEP 5 The purpose of Outlook's mail folders, shown in Figure 1.11, can be inferred from their names. The ***Outbox folder*** contains all of the messages you have written that have not yet been sent (uploaded) to the server. Once Outlook sends a message, it is automatically moved from the Outbox folder to the ***Sent Items folder***. This folder contains copies of messages that have been uploaded to the mail server. Messages will remain indefinitely in both the Inbox and Sent Items folders until you delete them, and then they are moved to the Deleted Items folder. If you close Outlook while you are in the midst of creating an email, Outlook saves the unfinished message in the ***Drafts folder***. If you are writing a long message, you can save it periodically and it will be stored in the Drafts folder. Unfinished messages can be opened from the Drafts folder, updated as needed, and then sent. Email is filtered as it comes into Outlook by the Junk Email Filter, which places messages suspected of being spam in the ***Junk Email folder***. Note that sometimes non-junk mail is routed to this folder, so it is a good idea to review this folder regularly.

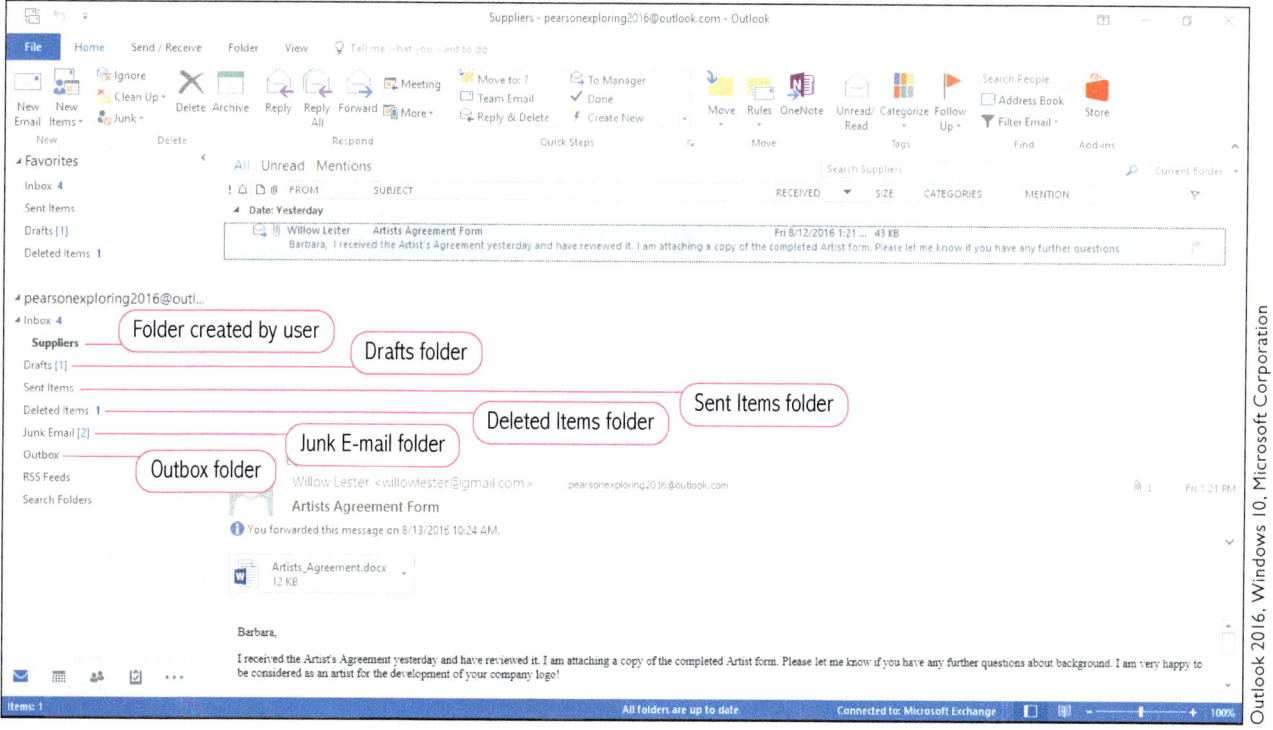

FIGURE 1.11 Mail Folders

Think about how you process your regular mail. You bring it into your house from the mailbox and read it at your leisure. Some mail is junk mail, which you immediately throw away. Other mail is important and you file it away with other important papers. And some mail you want to share with others in your household; you leave it on the kitchen table to reread at a later time.

Email is very similar. After you have been receiving email for some time, you will discover that by adding categories to your email, you can organize the various types of mail. You can organize your email further by creating folders with which to store the mail you receive. You can create folders in any of the mail folders, but most often, the Inbox is used.

To create a new folder, complete the following steps:

1. Click the Folder tab, and click New Folder in the New group.
2. Type a name for the folder in the Name box.
3. Confirm the type of items contained in the folder. For email, this will be Mail and Post Items.
4. Select the location where the new folder should appear in the *Select where to place the folder* list.
5. Click OK to finish creating the folder.

Folders appear in a hierarchical order. You can create folders within folders. For instance, you can create a Follow Up folder and add two folders to it, one to store mail from customers and another from suppliers. Only one email folder can be selected at a time (for example, the Suppliers folder shown in Figure 1.11), and its contents are displayed in the Outlook window.

You can move or copy messages from one mail folder to another. Follow the same conventions as you do in File Explorer; that is, drag a message from one folder to another.

Rules for automatically managing incoming email messages can be set up to move messages to a specified folder, play a sound, or display in a New Item Alert window based on criteria before you even see the message. Rules can be created using the sender's name, the subject, or to whom the message is sent. For instance, you could create a rule to cause any message from your supervisor to play a specific sound so that you will know to check your messages promptly.

To create a rule, complete the following steps:

1. Select the email message to which the rule will apply, and click Rules in the Move group on the Home tab.
2. Select Create Rule to open the Create Rule dialog box.
3. Click the check boxes to select the conditions you want to apply.
4. Select the check box you want to use and select the choices and options necessary to specify the actions you want.
5. Click OK to close the Create Rule dialog box.

You will possibly receive many unsolicited messages in your Inbox, just as you receive junk mail through the U.S. Post Office. In Outlook, your mail is filtered so that junk email does not appear as often in your Inbox, but you can also set up rules to block mail from certain senders.

Yet another option for managing email is to right-click on a message in the message list and select an option from the shortcut menu. Some of the options include Copy, Reply, Categorize, Follow up, Rules, Move, Quick Steps, Junk and Delete options.

Quick Steps are a convenient way to manage and organize email in your Inbox. They are found on the Home tab or on the shortcut menu. Multiple commands are compressed into a single click. Quick Steps differ from Rules in that they do not run automatically. You have to initiate a Quick Step by clicking a specific Quick Step command in the Quick

Steps group on the Home tab. Outlook provides predefined Quick Steps, or you can define your own steps. Quick Steps, for example, can move a message to a folder and mark it as read, or messages can be forwarded to a specific person with a single click. To use the Quick Steps, select the message in the Inbox, and click the Quick Step you would like to use from the Quick Steps group. The first time you use each Quick Step, a dialog box will prompt you through the setup, as shown in Figure 1.12. You can change the name of the item and the associated actions. Quick Steps are only available in the Mail component of Outlook.

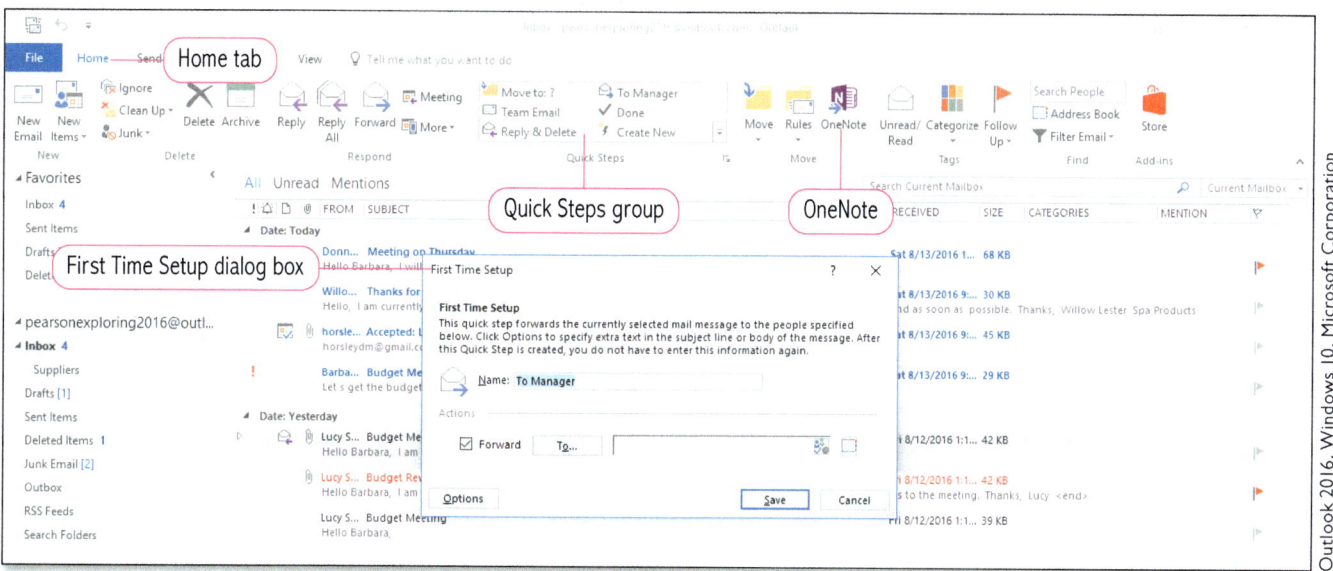

FIGURE 1.12 Quick Steps Dialog Box

There may be times when you want to retain a message for documentation or other reasons. OneNote is an application that enables you to take notes and save other types of information in a notebook. A selected message can be saved to a notebook by clicking OneNote in the Move group on the Home tab (refer to Figure 1.12). You can select the page or notebook where the message will be stored. The header will include the subject, who the message is from, the recipients, and the date it was sent, followed by the message text.

Mark Email for Follow Up

 You can flag messages for follow up at a later time. This adds a flag icon to the message to remind you visually to follow up, and it adds the follow up task to the To-Do Bar. With the message selected using POP3 or Exchange server, click Follow Up in the Tags group on the Home tab, and select the time frame Add Reminder, or Custom to specify additional parameters. When you have completed the follow up, click the flag icon, and it changes to a check to indicate that it is complete. If you are using IMAP, you can only set the flag, and cannot specify a time frame. You can only remove the flag when using IMAP to indicate that the follow up is complete.

1. Identify the various components of Outlook and describe their purpose. **pp. 5–9**
2. What types of files can be attached to an email message? **p. 16**
3. Describe a situation where you might forward a message. **p. 15**

Introduction to Outlook and Email • Outlook   19

Hands-On Exercises

Skills covered: Start Outlook • Send a Message • Read a Message • Reply to a Message • Attach a File • Open an Attachment • Create a New Folder • Store a Message in a Folder • Add a Signature to a Mail Message • Flag a Message for Follow Up • Manage the Mailbox

1 Introduction to Outlook and Email

Because your entrepreneurship team is busy, rather than meeting in person, it is most efficient to send email messages to communicate your ideas about your project. You decide to familiarize yourself with Outlook so that you can send messages and manage the replies that you receive. You plan to use Outlook when you start your professional career, so you decide to practice by using netiquette and other strategies for maintaining a professional appearance online.

STEP 1 » START OUTLOOK AND SEND A MESSAGE

After reading about the features and functions of Outlook, you are ready to jump in and experiment. You begin by familiarizing yourself with the Outlook interface. After your review, you focus on sending your first email message to one of your team members. You decide to send yourself a copy of the message, as a Bcc, so you can experiment with email in your Inbox at a later time. Refer to Figure 1.13 as you complete Step 1.

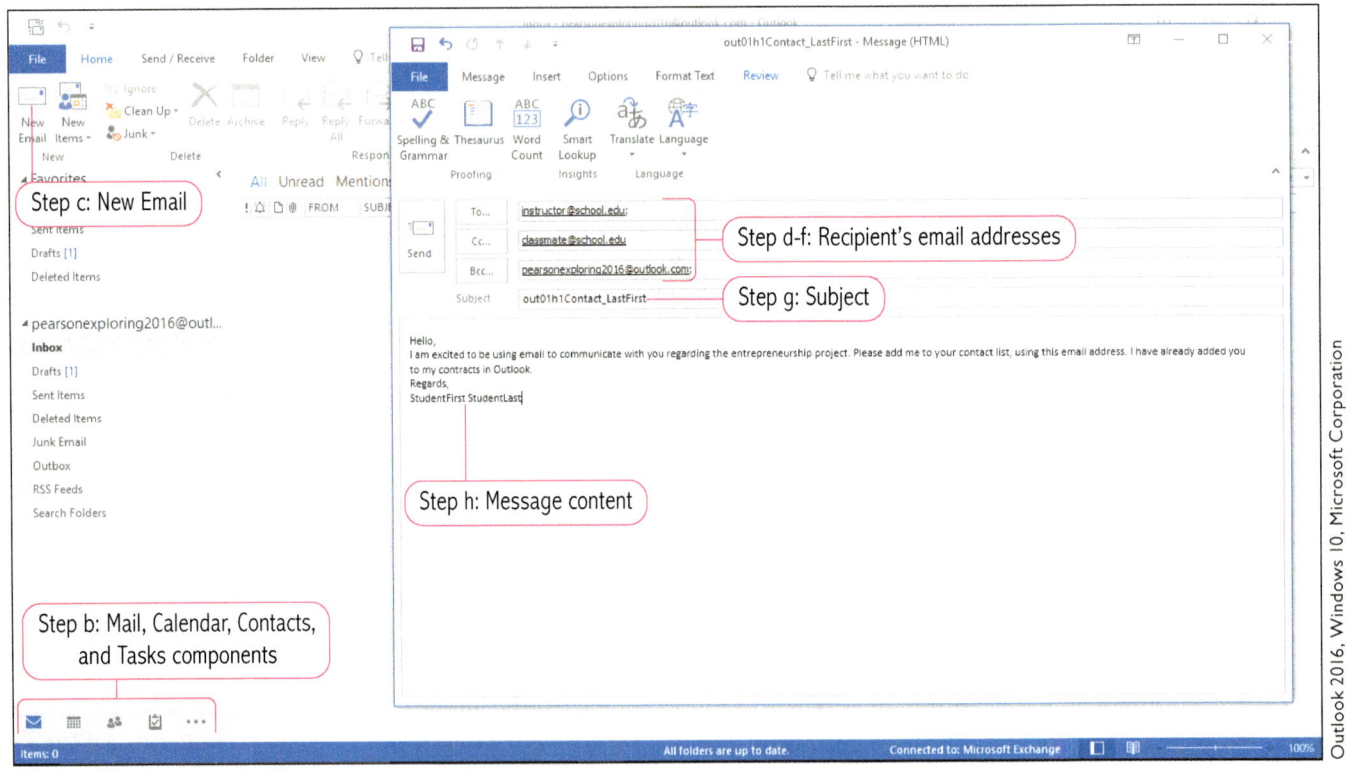

FIGURE 1.13 Send a Message

a. Start Outlook and maximize the Outlook window so it fills the entire desktop.

b. Review the parts of the Outlook window and confirm that you can find the items you read about in the chapter. Point to the task buttons at the bottom of the Folder Pane to glimpse the information for those components.

c. Click **New Email** in the New group on the Home tab to begin a new mail message.

d. Enter your instructor's email address in the To box.

> **TROUBLESHOOTING:** Double-check the addresses you enter into the address boxes for accuracy. Mail that is incorrectly addressed is not delivered by the mail server and will "bounce" back to your Inbox as undeliverable.

e. Press **Tab** to move the insertion point to the Cc box, and enter the email address of one of your classmates.

f. Ensure the Bcc box is displayed below the Cc box (click the Options tab and click Bcc in the Show Fields group). Press **Tab** to move the insertion point to the Bcc box. Enter your own email address so you will get a copy of the message.

You know you will automatically see a sent message in your Sent Items folder, but you would also like to have a message in your Inbox for experimentation.

g. Press **Tab** to move the insertion point to the Subject box. Type the subject line **out01h1Contact_ LastFirst**, as shown in Figure 1.13.

Use your last and first names. For example, as the Outlook author, I would use the subject line *out01h1Contact_StoverBarbara*.

h. Press **Tab** again to move to the message area. Enter the following text, pressing **Enter** only at the end of a paragraph. Use your first and last names at the end of the message.

Hello,

I am excited to be using email to communicate with you regarding the entrepreneurship project. Please add me to your contact list, using this email address. I have already added you to my contacts in Outlook.

Regards,

Your Name

i. Click the **Review tab**, and click **Spelling & Grammar** in the Proofing group. Correct any misspelled words. Click **OK** when the spelling check is complete. In addition, proofread your message, correcting any errors, and then click **Send**.

The message window closes automatically and you are returned to the normal view of Outlook.

STEP 2 » READ AND REPLY TO A MESSAGE

Knowing that you have sent a copy of the message to yourself, you access your mailbox and view the message. You will try the different views available to determine where you like to see the Reading Pane in the Outlook window. After reading the message, you decide to experiment with some of the other features of Outlook. You want to review email options, specifically to automatically check spelling before sending a message. Afterward, you will reply to a message to confirm your skills. Refer to Figure 1.14 as you complete Step 2.

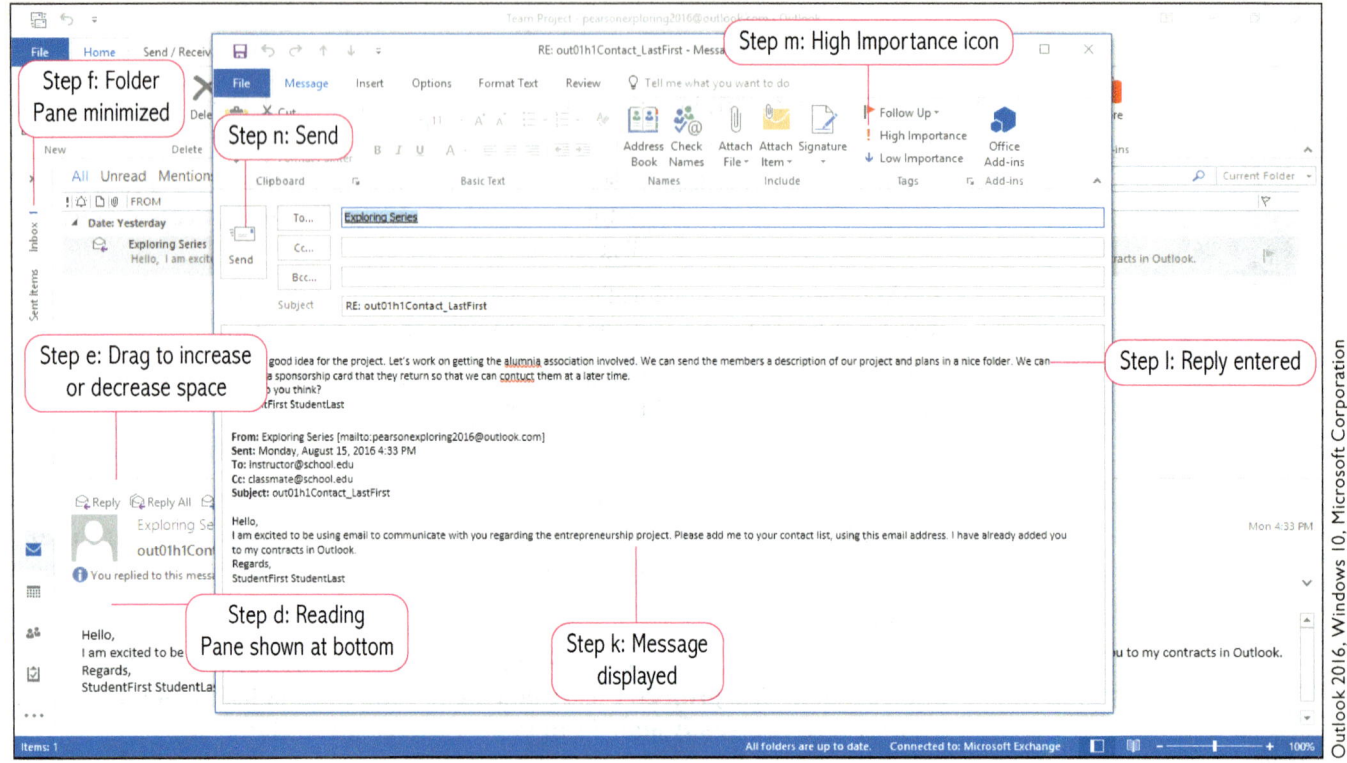

FIGURE 1.14 Reply to a Message

a. Wait a minute or two, click the **Send/Receive tab**, and then click **Send/Receive All Folders** in the Send & Receive group to retrieve your mail from the mail server.

> **TROUBLESHOOTING:** Email does not mean instant mail. It can take time for messages to be delivered through the server. Some servers may notify you as the messages arrive or add them to the message list without you having to click Send/Receive All Folders.

b. Click the **Inbox folder** on the Folder Pane. Click the **out01h1Contact_LastFirst subject line** for the message you sent to yourself.

c. Click the **View tab**, click **Reading Pane** in the Layout group, and then click **Right** to display the message on the right side of the window.

The selected message is displayed in the Reading Pane.

d. Click **Reading Pane**, and click **Bottom**.

The selected message is displayed in the bottom half of the window (see Figure 1.14). You may have to scroll down to see the all of the message.

e. Drag the top edge of the Reading Pane upward to enlarge its size so that you can see more of the message. Drag the top edge downward to return it to the previous size.

By default, you can only change the size of the Reading Pane so much. This way, you never completely lose your Folder Pane, folder message display, or Reading Pane.

f. Click **Folder Pane** in the Layout group, and click **Off** to remove the Folder Pane so that you can see more of the message.

g. Press **Alt+F1** to display the Folder Pane again.

Alt+F1 works as a toggle switch to open and close the Folder Pane.

h. Click the **File tab**. Click **Options** in the left pane to display the Outlook Options dialog box. Ensure that Mail is selected in the left pane.

Familiarize yourself with the options you can modify using the dialog box. Be sure to scroll down the dialog box, as there are many options. Limit your review to just the Mail options at this time.

i. Click the **Always check spelling before sending check box** in the *Compose messages* section to select it. Keep the check in the Ignore original message text in reply or forward.

Each time you send a message, the spelling will be checked, but when you reply to a message, only the text that you type will be checked for correct spelling.

j. Click **OK** to close the dialog box.

k. Double-click the message you sent to yourself in the message list. Click **Reply**.

There are multiple ways to initiate a reply. You can use the Ribbon, click on the icon in the message header, or right-click on a message in the message list and select Reply. The insertion point is in the bottom Reading pane at the top of the message.

l. Enter the following text as the reply to the message. Note that the misspelled words are intentional. You are being asked to type incorrectly spelled words purposely (refer to Figure 1.14) so you can experiment with the Spelling feature. Type them exactly as they are displayed, incorrectly spelled. Do not correct them at this time.

Use your first and last names at the end of the message.

Hi Jake,

I have a good idea for the project. Let's work on getting the alumnia association involved. We can send the members a description of our project and plans in a nice folder. We can include a sponsorship card that they return so that we can contuct them at a later time.

What do you think?

Your Name

m. Click **High Importance** in the Tags group.

The High Importance symbol (a red exclamation point) will display when the message appears in the recipient's Inbox.

n. Click **Send** when you complete your reply. The words that are misspelled appear, one at a time, in the Spelling dialog box. Select the correct spelling of each word, and click **Change**. Once the spelling is completely corrected, the message is sent.

TROUBLESHOOTING: If a word is spelled correctly but it is flagged as incorrect (such as proper nouns or other words not found in the dictionary), click Ignore in the dialog box. If the correct spelling is not shown in the Suggestions box, select the misspelled word displayed in the sentence at the top of the dialog box and correct the spelling.

---

o. Close the out01h1Contact_LastFirst message.

STEP 3 » ATTACH A FILE AND OPEN AN ATTACHMENT

You know that you will have many attachments to send to your teammates and others as you move forward with your project. You will experiment with sending a file to your instructor. You decide to open the copy of the message you sent to yourself and confirm that the attachment worked. Refer to Figure 1.15 as you complete Step 3.

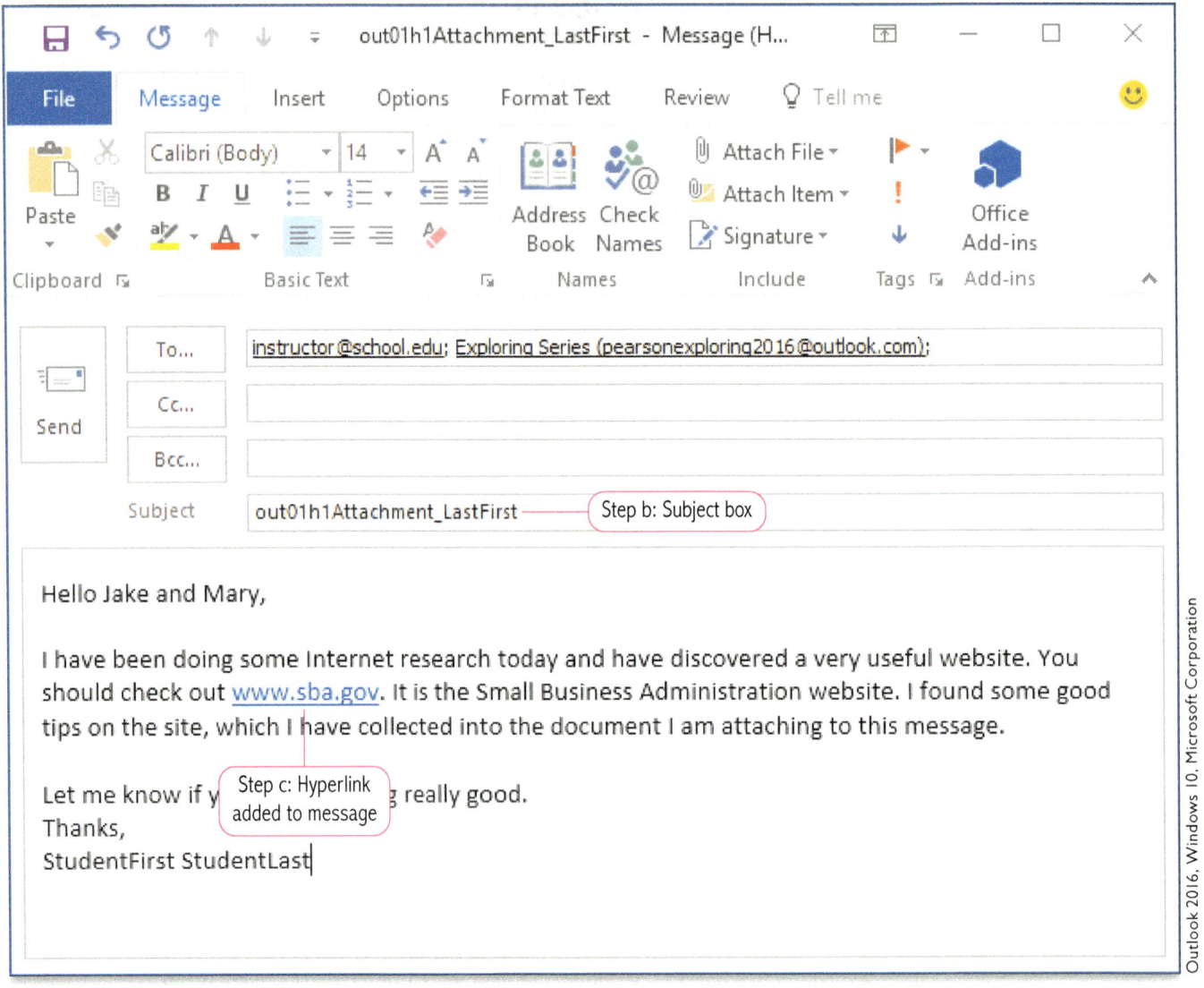

FIGURE 1.15 Add an Attachment

a. Click the Home tab and click **New Email** in the New group. Enter your instructor's email address in the **To box**, followed by a semicolon, and then enter your own email address.

> **TROUBLESHOOTING:** If a ScreenTip pops up as you are typing the name, you can click the name, or press Tab, if it is the one you want and it will automatically complete the entry, placing a semicolon after the name.

b. Click in the **Subject box**, and type **out01h1Attachment_LastFirst** for the subject line.

c. Press **Tab**, and type the text shown in Figure 1.15, being sure to enter the Web address exactly as shown: **www.sba.gov**. Press **Enter** twice after each paragraph to insert a blank line as shown in the figure. Include your first and last names at the end of the message.

The Web address changes to a hyperlink as soon as you press Enter or space. The message recipient can click the hyperlink to open the webpage in a browser.

d. Click **Attach File** in the Include group to display the Insert File dialog box. Click **Browse this PC** at the bottom of the Recent Items list. Navigate to the student data files and select the Word file **out01h1Ideas**. Click **Insert** to attach the selected file to your message.

You will see the name of the file in the Attached box, below the Subject line. You can also attach a file by dragging it from the File Explorer window to the message box.

e. Click **Send**. Correct any spelling errors that are displayed.

The editing window closes automatically, and you are returned to the Inbox folder.

f. Wait a minute or two, and retrieve your mail from the mail server. Double-click the message **out01h1Attachment_LastFirst** you just sent in the message list to open it.

The Web address you entered in Step c appears as a hyperlink. It will display in purple or blue, depending on whether you have already visited the webpage or not.

g. Click **www.sba.gov** to ensure the hyperlink works properly. The browser should display the webpage. Close the browser window when you have confirmed that the link opened correctly.

TROUBLESHOOTING: If the webpage does not appear, you may have incorrectly typed the Web address in the email message. Also, your computer must be connected to the Internet in order to display webpages.

h. Click the **out01h1Ideas** attachment to preview the content.

Clicking the attachment opens a preview window for reading, and avoids having to open the related application. In order to edit the file, you must open the file in the related application.

TROUBLESHOOTING: If the file opened in the software application, you double-clicked the attachment. Close the application once you have reviewed the contents of the attachment.

i. Click the **Back to message** arrow above the attachment display after reading the content of the file. Close the email message, and return to the Inbox folder.

STEP 4 » ADD SIGNATURES TO MAIL MESSAGES

You would like to make your email messages more distinctive, while preserving a professional look. You create signatures to achieve this purpose. Refer to Figure 1.16 as you complete Step 4.

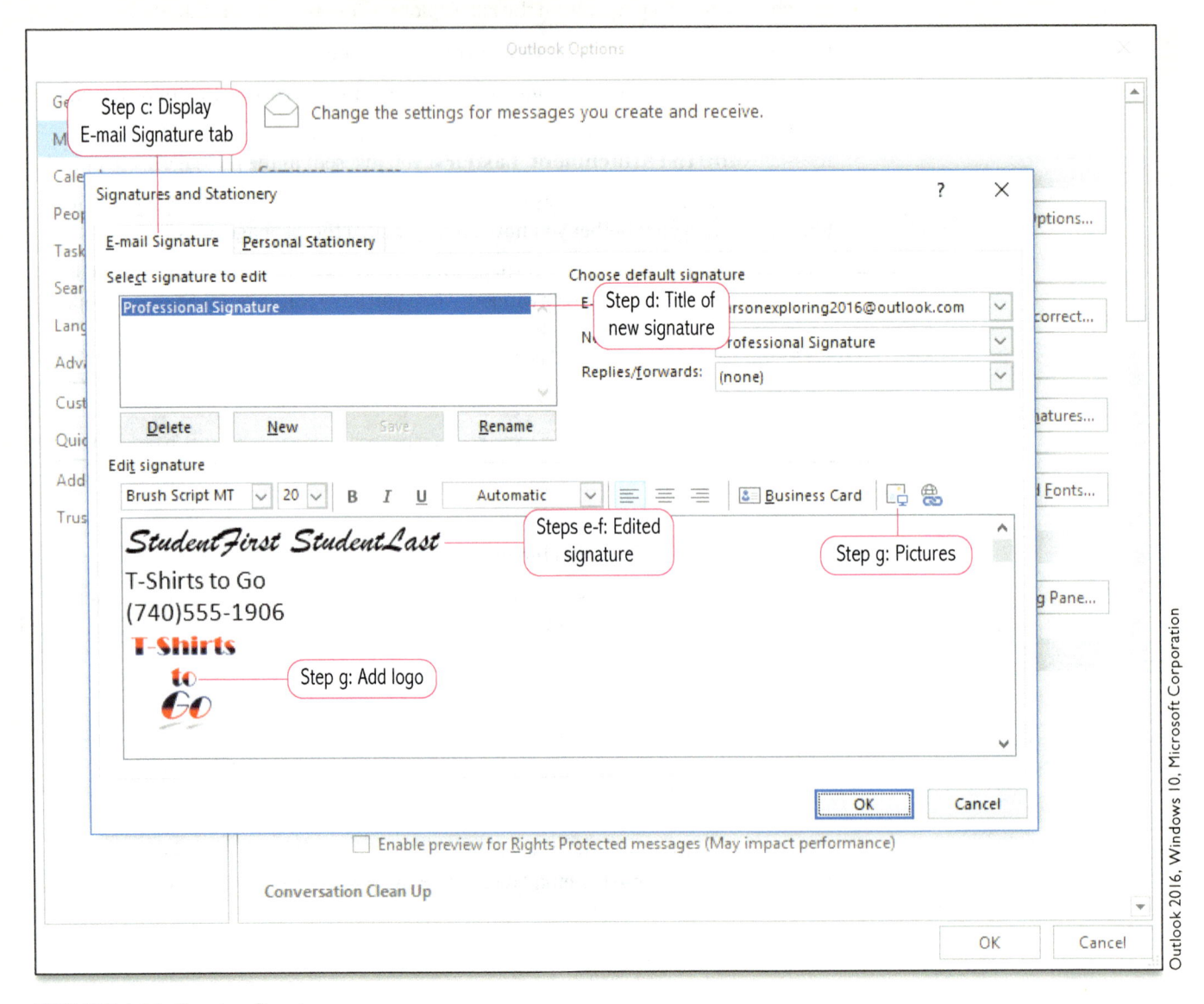

FIGURE 1.16 Create a Signature

a. Click the **File tab**. Click **Options** in the left pane to display the Outlook Options dialog box. Click **Mail** in the left pane.

b. Click the **Compose messages in this format arrow**, and select **HTML**, if it is not already selected.

c. Click **Signatures** in the *Compose messages* section. The Signatures and Stationery dialog box opens with two tabs. Ensure the E-mail Signature tab is selected.

d. Click **New**, enter **Professional Signature** in the *Type a name for this signature* box, and then click **OK**.

e. Enter your first and last name in the Edit Signature box, and press **Enter**. Select the text you typed. Click the **Font arrow** and select **Brush Script MT**. Increase the font size to **20**.

f. Click on the next line of the Edit Signature box, change the font to **Calibri** size **14**, and then type **T-Shirts to Go**. Press **Enter**, and type **(740)555-1906**. Press **Enter**.

CHAPTER 1 • Hands-On Exercise 1

g. Click **Pictures** (to the right of Business Card), navigate to the student data files, and then select *out01h1Logo.png*. Click **Insert**. Click **OK** to close the Signatures and Stationery dialog box. Click **OK** to close the Outlook Options dialog box.

h. Click **New Email** on the Home tab to open a new message window. The message is formatted with the signature you created. Compose a message to yourself and your instructor for use in the next step. Use the Subject line **out01h1Reflections_LastFirst**. In the message, discuss the things you have learned so far about Outlook.

i. Click **Send**.

STEP 5 » CREATE A NEW FOLDER AND STORE A MESSAGE IN THE FOLDER

As you begin to send and receive messages in your email account, you realize that efficient organization of those messages is going to be very important. You decide to create a folder to store correspondence with your teammates and others involved in your entrepreneurship project. Refer to Figure 1.17 as you complete Step 5.

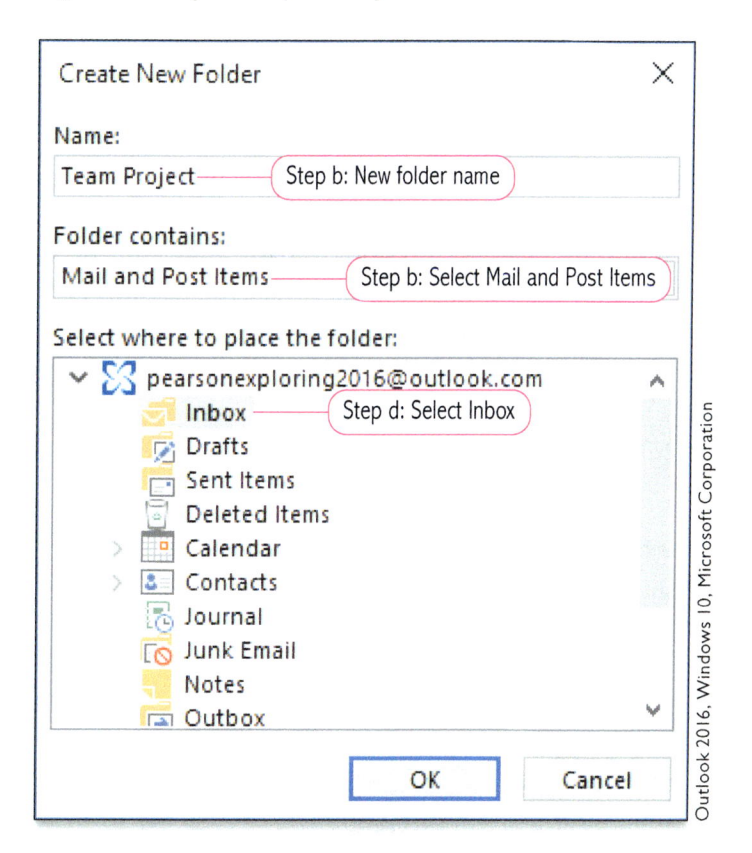

FIGURE 1.17 Create a Folder

a. Click the **Folder tab**, and click **New Folder** in the New group to display the Create New Folder dialog box shown in Figure 1.17.

b. Enter **Team Project** in the Name box. Ensure that the *Folder contains* box has Mail and Post Items selected.

c. Select **Inbox** in the *Select where to place the folder* section to place the new folder in the Inbox. Click **OK** to create the new folder.

A new folder will display under Inbox in the Folder Pane of the Inbox window.

TROUBLESHOOTING: If the new folder does not display, click the Expand arrow to the left of the Inbox folder on the Folder Pane to display the folders within the Inbox.

Hands-On Exercise 1   27

d. Click **Inbox** on the Folder Pane, select the first message in the Inbox message list that you created in this exercise with the subject **win01h1Contact_LastFirst**, and then move it to the Team Project folder in the folder list.

e. Click the **Team Project folder** in the Folder Pane to open the folder.

The message that you dragged to the Team Project folder is displayed in the message list, whereas the name in the Title bar of the Outlook window changes to Team Project–Personal Folders (or your email address) – Outlook.

f. Click the **Inbox folder** in the Folder Pane to return to your Inbox.

STEP 6 » FLAG A MESSAGE FOR FOLLOW UP AND ORGANIZE MESSAGES

Some messages that you receive may need to be put aside until you obtain more information. You will experiment with flagging messages. You will also organize messages using a Quick Step. Refer to Figures 1.18 and 1.19 as you complete Step 6.

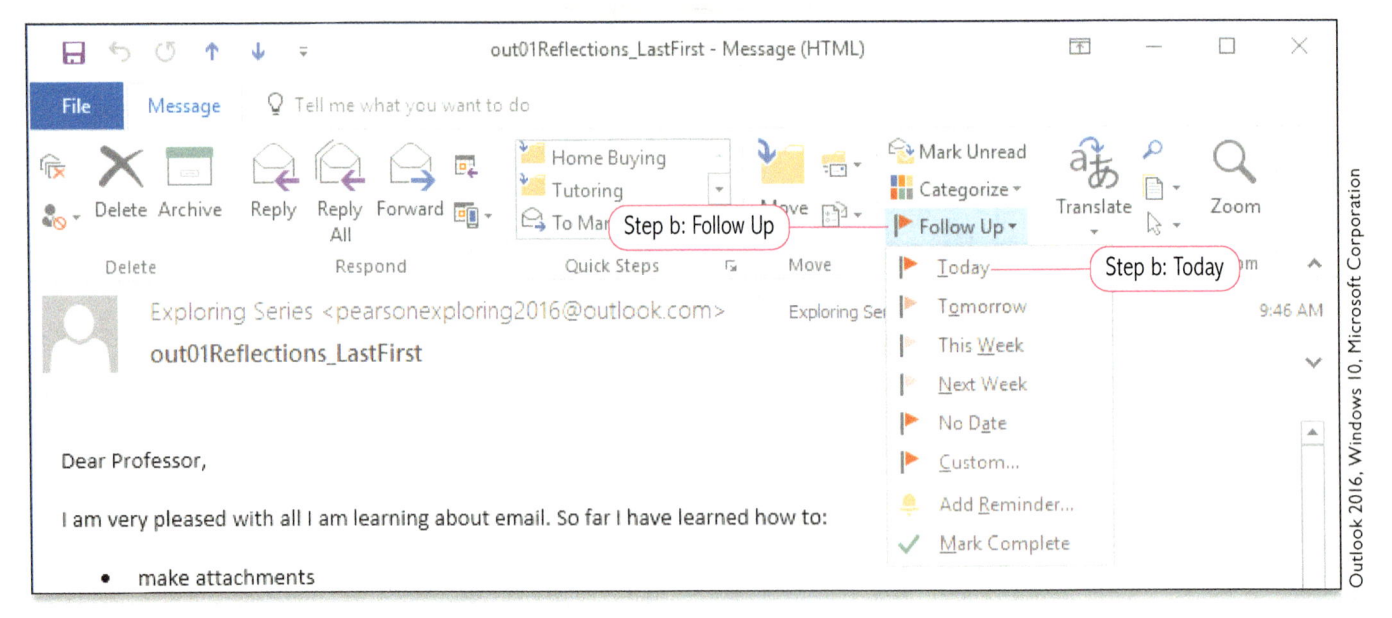

FIGURE 1.18 Flag a Message (Exchange Server)

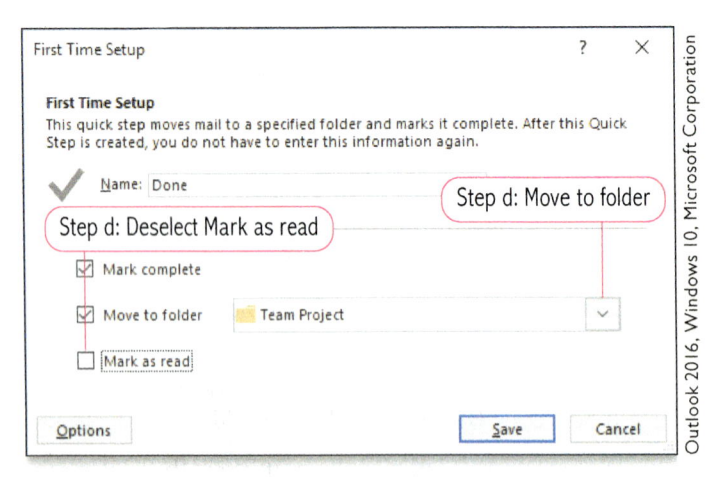

FIGURE 1.19 Quick Step First Time Setup Dialog Box

28 CHAPTER 1 • Hands-On Exercise 1

a. Retrieve your message from the mail server. Select the message with the subject **out01h1Reflections_LastFirst** that you sent in Step 4 in the message list.

b. Click **Follow Up** in the Tags group. If you are using an Exchange server or POP3 account, you have additional options for setting reminders when you use the Follow Up command, click **Today**, or if you are using an IMAP account, click **Flag Message**.

A red flag will display in the message list indicating a follow up is due today.

c. Ensure that the message that you sent in Step 4 with the subject **out01h1Reflections_LastFirst** is selected in the message list. Click **Done** in the Quick Steps group.

> **TROUBLESHOOTING:** If you do not see the First Time Setup dialog box, right-click Done in the Quick Steps group and select Edit Done.

> **TROUBLESHOOTING:** If you do not see the Done Quick Step, click Create New, type Done as the Quick Step name, and click the Choose an Action arrow. Select Move to folder to continue with the next step.

d. Click the **Move to folder arrow** and select the **Team Project** folder. Deselect **Mark as read**. Click **Save**.

The action for the Quick Step Done button is modified to send the message to the Team Project folder. This is a one-time set up for this button.

> **TROUBLESHOOTING:** If you do not see an option to Mark as read, click Options, click Add action, and then select the Mark as read option. Click Finish after changing the settings.

e. Click **Done** in the Quick Steps group. Click the **Team Project folder** in the Folders Pane and ensure the message has moved to the folder.

f. Open the Snipping Tool and click **New** (in the Snipping Tool application). Take a screenshot of the Team Project folder and message list. Save the snip as **out01h1TeamFolder_LastFirst**. You will submit this file to your instructor at the end of Hands-On Exercise 3.

g. Keep Outlook onscreen if you plan to continue with Hands-On Exercise 2. Exit Outlook if you do not want to continue with the next exercise at this time.

Outlook Contacts

Just about everyone you know has an email address. The Contacts component of Outlook enables you to keep track of the addresses. When it is time to send an email message to one of your contacts, you can select the recipient from your Contacts folder without having to type his or her entire email address. Click Contacts on the Folder Pane to view your Contacts list. You can change the Contacts view to display the information in a way that suits you. You can also assign your contacts to categories and color-code them. Contact Groups enable you to send email quickly to a predefined group of people. You will find that keeping track of people using Outlook Contacts can be pretty helpful.

In this section, you will learn how to add contacts in Outlook. You will organize your contacts by category and color-code them. You will create a Contact Group to send email to a group of people and send the group an email message.

Managing Contacts

STEP 1 The information about each person in Contacts is entered into a contact card, as shown in Figure 1.20. You can enter as much or as little information as you want, but generally, you will at least enter a name and email address. It is in this window that you select the categories, if any, to which contacts are assigned.

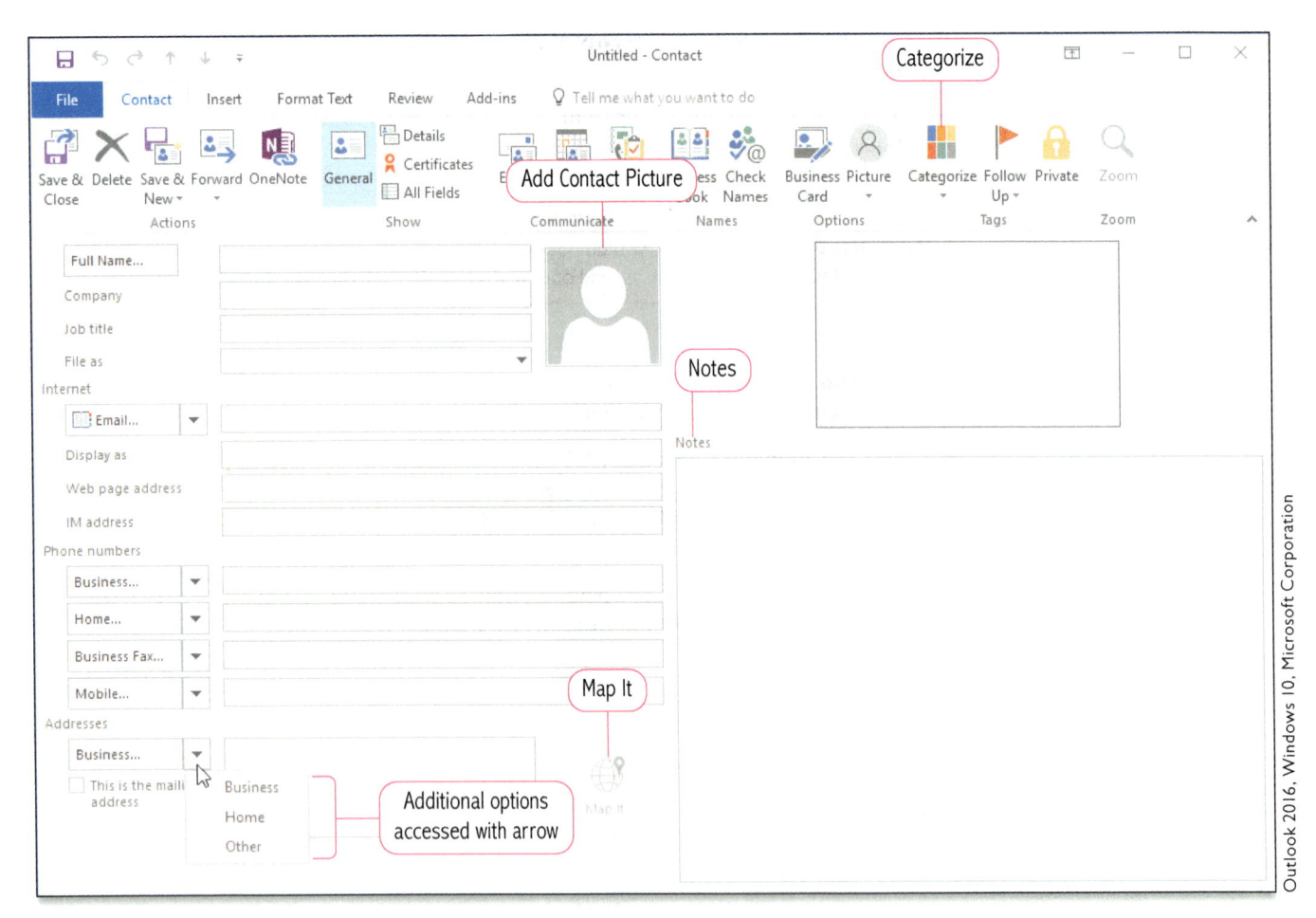

FIGURE 1.20 New Contact Window

> **TIP: MAP IT**
> When you enter an address onto a contact card, the Map It feature of Outlook Contacts activates. Click Map It on the contact card to see a Bing.com map with the address marked.

30   CHAPTER 1 • Managing Email, Contacts, Tasks, and Calendars

As Figure 1.20 shows, the contact card is very flexible in that it enables you to enter more than one email and/or address for each person. It also has fields for multiple phone numbers, Internet addresses, and postal addresses, a necessity in this world, where everyone is connected 24/7. You can add notes in the box at the right of the dialog box.

Photographs of your contacts can be added to their contact cards, making it easy to identify the contact you need when using the Business Card view. You can add a photograph to the contact card as you create it, or return to the card and add it later. Click Add Contact Picture, represented by the People icon on the contact card. Locate the photograph, and click OK. Later, when you receive an email message from the contact, you will see the picture rather than the People icon in the header of the message.

> **TIP: THE PEOPLE ICON**
>
> If you are using an Exchange server, the People icon, displayed in the header of the message, enables you to select different ways to contact the sender of the message. Contacts where you have added a photograph will display the picture in the message header. Depending on whether you have contact information stored, you can select to send a message, use instant messaging, or even dial a phone number.

Change Views

As with other Outlook components, the Contacts folder can be customized to your needs. The various views enable you to work in a natural way. In Figure 1.6 at the beginning of this chapter, you saw the Business Cards view of the Contacts folder. You can also view the contact information in People view, as Business Cards or Cards, in a Phone listing, and as a List. The People view shows a pane on the left with all of the contact names and pictures, while on the right, the selected contact's information is displayed in the Reading Pane, as shown in Figure 1.21. The Reading Pane can be on the right, at the bottom, or turned off.

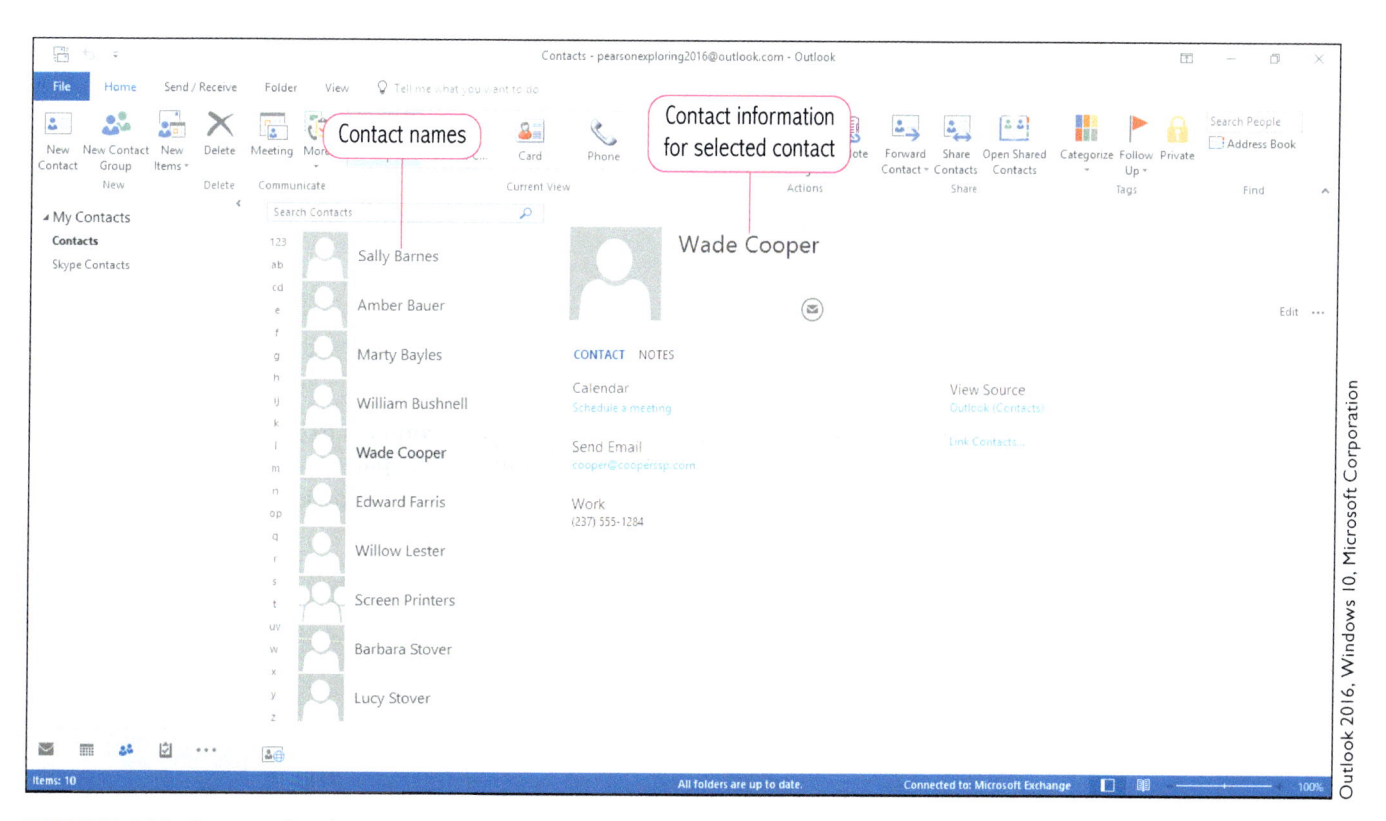

FIGURE 1.21 Contacts Displayed in People View

The Business Card view shows the contact information for all of your contacts in a larger view of each card than the Card view. The Card view displays more cards, and enables you to select the contact you wish to view more efficiently. Double-click the card to display the contact's complete information. The Phone view displays a list that focuses on the available phone numbers in the Contacts list by placing the phone numbers in columns.

You can modify views to display just the type of information you are most likely to need. Click the More button in the Current View group, and select Manage Views. Select the View you want to modify, and click Modify to open the Advanced View Settings dialog box. Depending on the view, you can modify columns displayed, grouping, sort order, filtering, and more as shown in Figure 1.22. You can reset the view to the original configuration by clicking Reset View in the Current View group on the View tab.

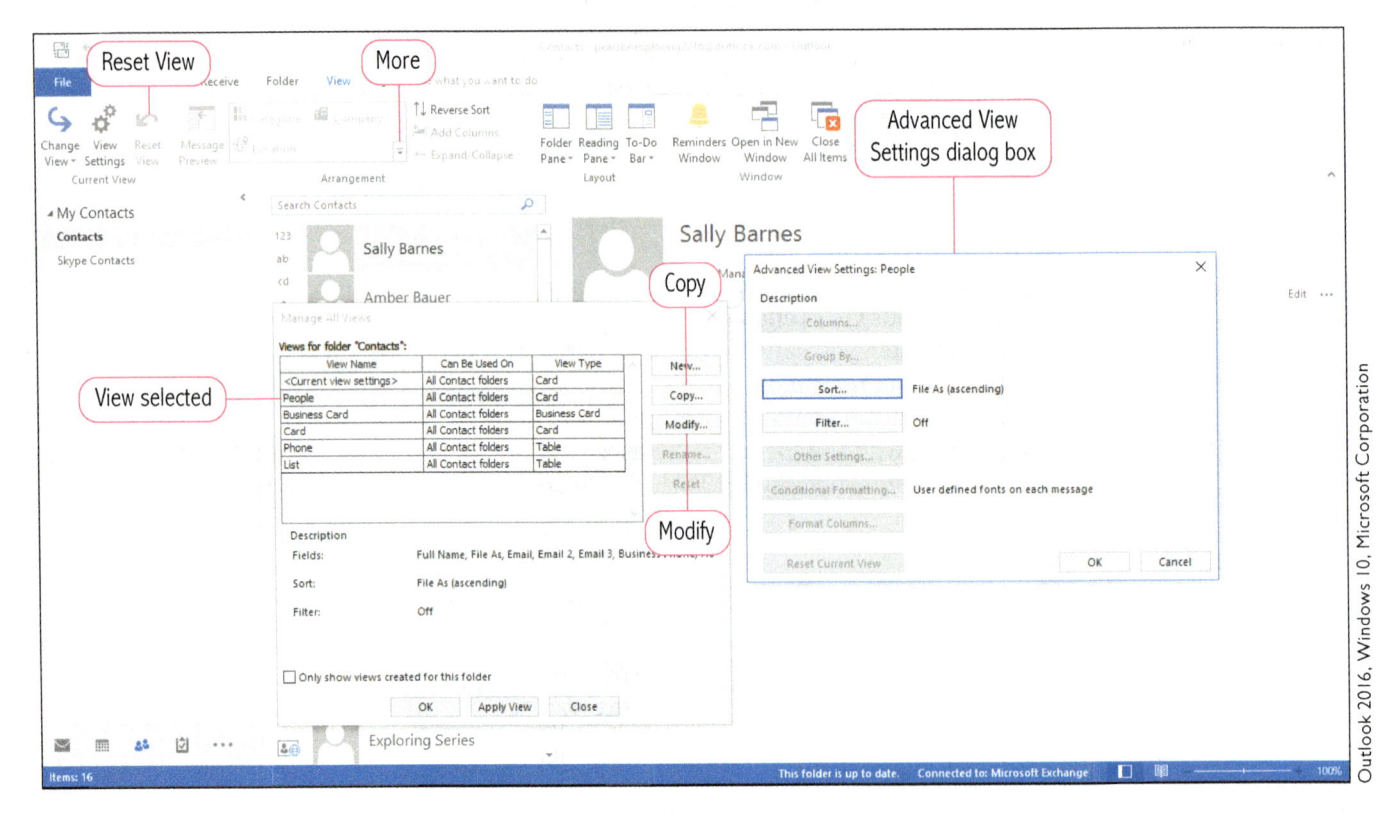

FIGURE 1.22 Manage a View

Organize Contacts

STEP 2
STEP 3

Categories in Outlook enable you to assign your contacts to color-coded categories and then view contacts in a Phone list or List view by category arrangement, as shown in Figure 1.23. A person can be assigned to more than one category.

32   CHAPTER 1 • Managing Email, Contacts, Tasks, and Calendars

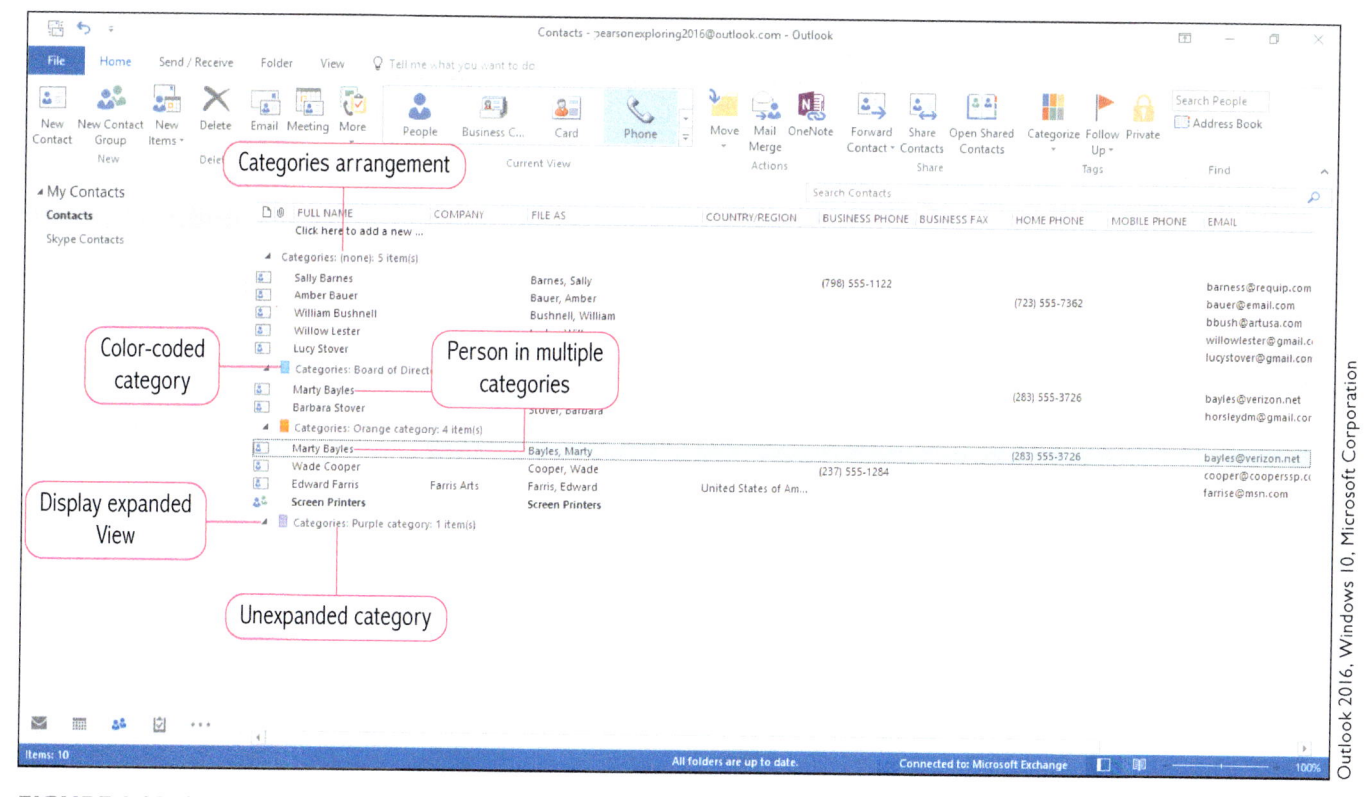

FIGURE 1.23 Contacts Viewed by Categories

Note also that you can sort the contacts within categories by clicking a field at the top of the Contacts list. For instance, should you want to see all of your contacts within a particular organization, you could click the Company field. Toggling the Display Expanded View arrow expands and contracts the entries within it.

Outlook Contacts enable you to organize your contacts another way that is very useful for keeping in touch with teammates on group projects. You can set up a Contact Group, or distribution list, as shown in Figure 1.24. Once the list is set up, you can send email to the entire list at once by entering the list name in the address box in a new message. You can also notify the entire distribution list at one time of a meeting you are trying to arrange or assign everyone on the list to a task. Once established, your distribution list will display in your Contact Group in alphabetical order with the rest of the Contact names.

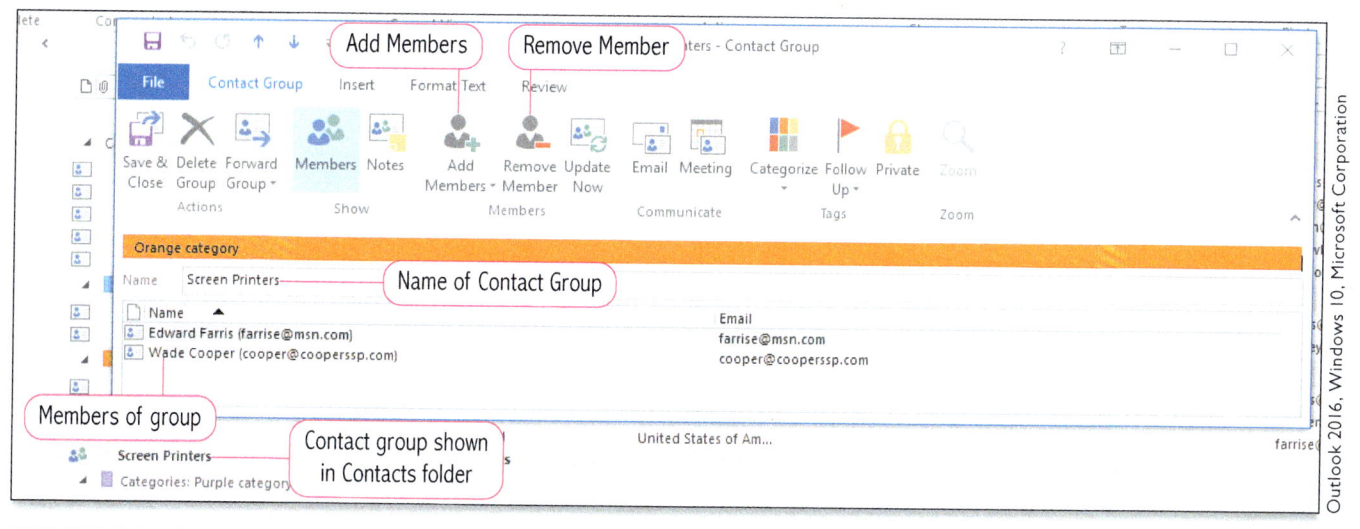

FIGURE 1.24 Contact Group Dialog Box

Outlook Contacts • Outlook   33

Use Contacts

STEP 4 ▶▶ Once you have established Contacts, you can select the person or group with which you want to communicate and click the appropriate button in the Communicate group on the Home tab, as shown in Figure 1.25. You can send an email to the selected people (or groups), or include them in a meeting invitation. Click More to assign a task or make a phone call to a selected individual.

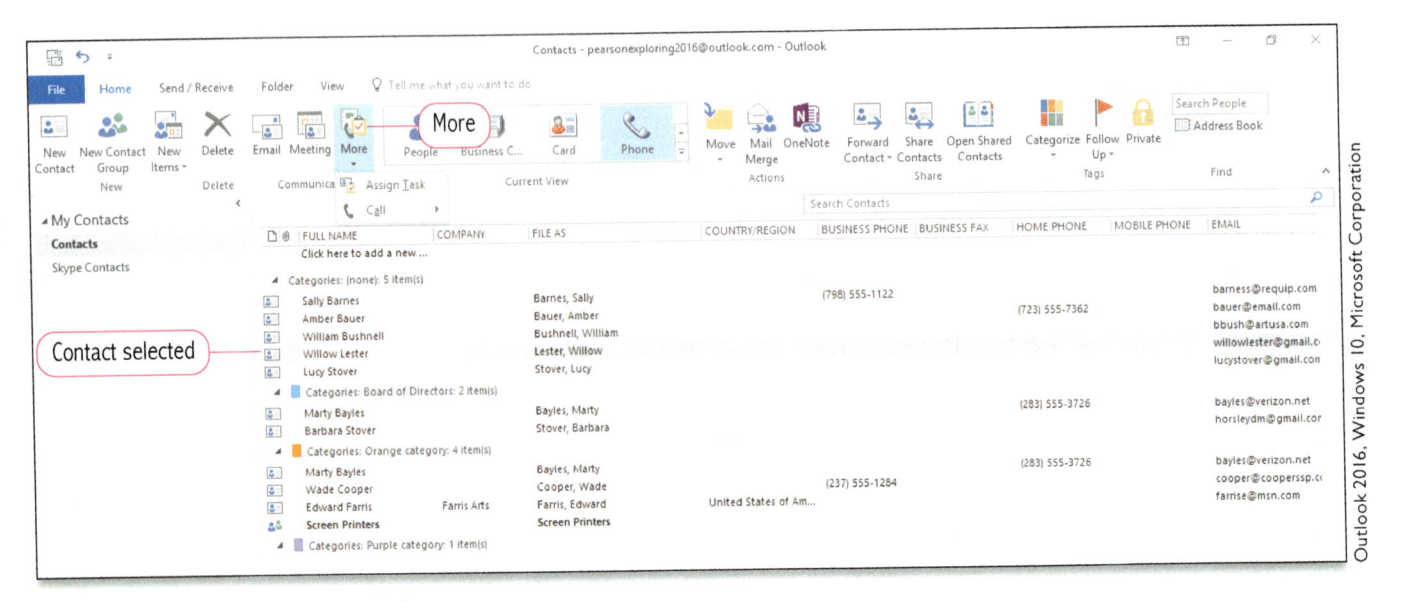

FIGURE 1.25 Communicate with Contacts

TIP: CREATE A BACKUP
It is a good idea to maintain a backup copy of your email, contacts, and calendar. Periodically, you should copy the Outlook data file (.pst) to a different location such as a flash drive or external disk drive. On Backstage view, use Import/Export on the Open & Export screen to save the file. You can also use this option to import contacts from a different email account that you may have.

Quick Concepts

4. Explain how the Contacts List is useful when sending email. ***p. 30***
5. Describe the difference between categories and groups. ***pp. 32–33***

34 CHAPTER 1 • Managing Email, Contacts, Tasks, and Calendars

Hands-On Exercises

Skills covered: Create a Contact List • Add a Contact Category • Change the Contacts View • Organize Contacts • Create a Contact Group • Use the Contact Group to Send Email • Print Contacts as a PDF File

2 Outlook Contacts

You are quickly finding out that managing all the information about people who are involved in the entrepreneurship project is overwhelming. You decide to maintain a contact list for every person related to the project and to organize them into categories. You think that it might be a good idea to market your T-shirts by sending email to a list of prospects informing them of where they can purchase the T-shirts.

STEP 1 » CREATE A CONTACT LIST

You will set up contacts so that you can quickly find information such as phone numbers, email addresses, and addresses. Refer to Figure 1.26 as you complete Step 1.

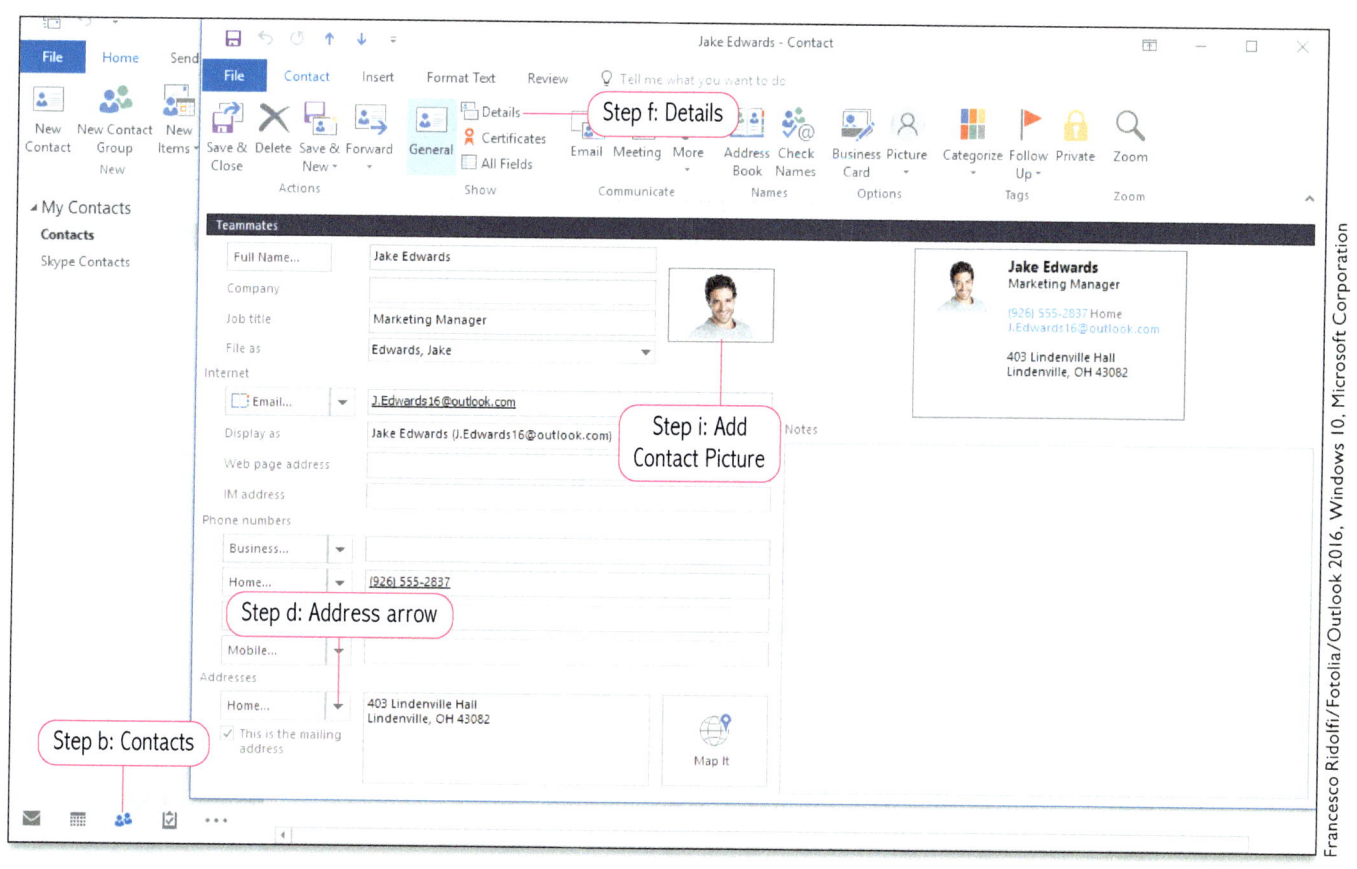

FIGURE 1.26 Create a Contact List

Hands-On Exercise 2   35

a. Open Outlook if you closed it at the end of Hands-On Exercise 1. Ensure that the Folder Pane is displayed on the left side of the window.

> **TROUBLESHOOTING:** If you do not see the Folder Pane, select the View tab, click Folder Pane in the Layout group, and then click Normal.

b. Click **Contacts** at the bottom of the Folder Pane. Click **New Contact** in the New group on the Home tab to open the Contact card.

c. Enter the contact information for Mary Taylor.

- Full name: **Mary Taylor**
- Job title: **Production Manager**
- Email: **marytaylor@email.com**
- Home phone number: **387-555-3482**

As you type the contact information, some field entries, such as for the *File as* and the *Display as* fields, will automatically display. You will see the contact card fill with information as you complete the fields and move to the next.

d. Click the **Addresses arrow** in the Addresses section, and select **Home**.

e. Click in the **address box**, type **124 Winter St.**, press **Enter**, and then type **Lindenville, OH 43287**.

f. Click **Details** in the Show group on the Contact tab. Type **Production** in the Department box.

g. Click **General** in the Show group to display the contact card. Review the information on the contact card to ensure that it is correct. Click **Save & Close** in the Actions group.

h. Click **New Contact** in the New group again, and add the following information to a contact card for Jake Edwards.

- Full name: **Jake Edwards**
- Job title: **Marketing Manager**
- Email: **J.Edwards16@outlook.com**
- Home phone number: **926-555-2837**
- Home address: **403 Lindenville Hall, Lindenville, OH 43802**

i. Click **Add Contact Picture**, navigate to the student data files, and then select *out01h2ContactPhoto*. Click **OK**. Click **Save & Close** in the Actions group.

The photo of the contact now appears on the Contact card and in the Business Card view.

j. Continue adding classmates and your instructor to the contact list until you have four or five entries. For each contact card, include at least the person's name and email address. Also, create a contact with your information (real or fictional), providing your name, email address, home (or mobile) phone number, home address, and birth date.

STEP 2 » ADD A CONTACT CATEGORY AND CHANGE THE CONTACTS VIEW

By adding contact categories, you can quickly find contacts that have some sort of relationship. For instance, you may create a personal contacts category and a business contacts category. To assist you in organizing your contacts for the team project, you decide to organize your suppliers into one category and your teammates into another. You wish to experiment with the various Contacts views. Refer to Figure 1.27 as you complete Step 2.

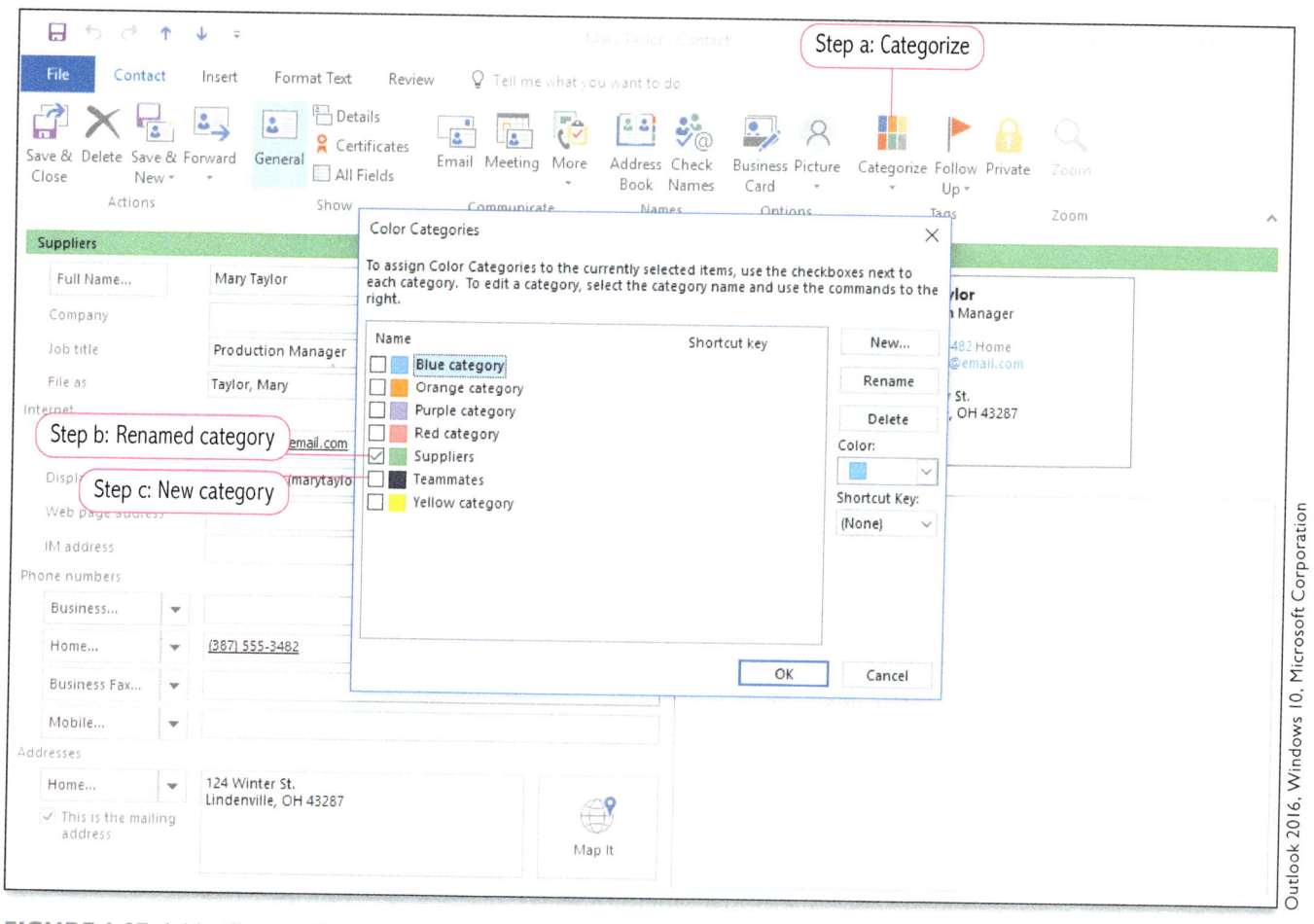

FIGURE 1.27 Add a Contact Category

a. Click **Phone** in the Current View group on the Home tab. Double-click the contact for Mary Taylor in the Contacts list. Click **Categorize** in the Tags group, and click **All Categories** to display the dialog box shown in Figure 1.27.

b. Select the **Green Category**, and click **Rename**. Type **Suppliers**. Press **Enter** to accept the change. Click the **Suppliers check box** to select it and add Mary to the category.

c. Click **New**. Type **Teammates** in the Name box. Use the **Color arrow** to select **Dark Blue** for the category. Click **OK**.

> **TROUBLESHOOTING:** The color names appear as a ScreenTip when the pointer hovers over each color block on the palette.

Hands-On Exercise 2   37

d. Click the **Teammates check box** for Mary to deselect it, and click **OK**.

Mary will be in the Suppliers category only. The Teammates category will be used later for other contacts.

e. Click **Save & New** in the Actions group to save the information for the supplier and simultaneously open a new Contact window.

> **TROUBLESHOOTING:** If you clicked Save & Close by mistake, click New Contact on the Home tab in the New group.

f. Create a new contact entry for another classmate by entering their full name, email address, home phone number, and home address. Fictional information is acceptable for this entry.

g. Click **Details** in the Show group, and enter a birth date into the Birthday list box (a fictional date is acceptable). If you are asked to save the contact information, click **OK**.

h. Click **Categorize** in the Tags group, and add this person to the Teammates category. Click **Save & Close** in the Actions group.

When you open the calendar in Hands-On Exercise 3, your teammate's birthday will be listed as an event on the appropriate date.

i. Click **Jake Edwards** in the Contacts list. Click **Categorize** in the Tags group. Click the **Teammates category** to select it.

j. Assign two other people to the Suppliers category. Assign your personal contact card to the Teammates category.

k. Click **More** in the Current View group, and click **Card**.

The gallery of Current Views opens so that you may select Card.

l. Click the letter **T** in the alphabetic index.

The first address card of the person whose name begins with the letter *T* is selected. This is an efficient way to move through multiple contacts.

m. Double-click Mary Taylor's contact card. Mary's phone number is incorrect. Click Mary's phone number, highlight the number, and then type **387-555-3982**. Close Mary's contact card.

> **TROUBLESHOOTING:** If you cannot find the contact card for Mary Taylor, click the Search Contacts box, and type the name Taylor. Press Enter and that contact will be shown in the Contact window. Close the search by clicking Close in the Search Contacts area. If you have two contacts with the same last name, a dialog box will appear that requests that you select the contact you wish to see. Click OK and the Contact dialog box will open.

n. Click **Phone** in the Current View group to display the contacts in phone list order.

STEP 3 ❯❯ ORGANIZE YOUR CONTACTS AND CREATE A CONTACT GROUP

Again, realizing that how you organize your contacts will dictate how quickly you can find certain people, you decide to experiment with the various views and filters available in Outlook. You will also create a Contact Group. Refer to Figure 1.28 as you complete Step 3.

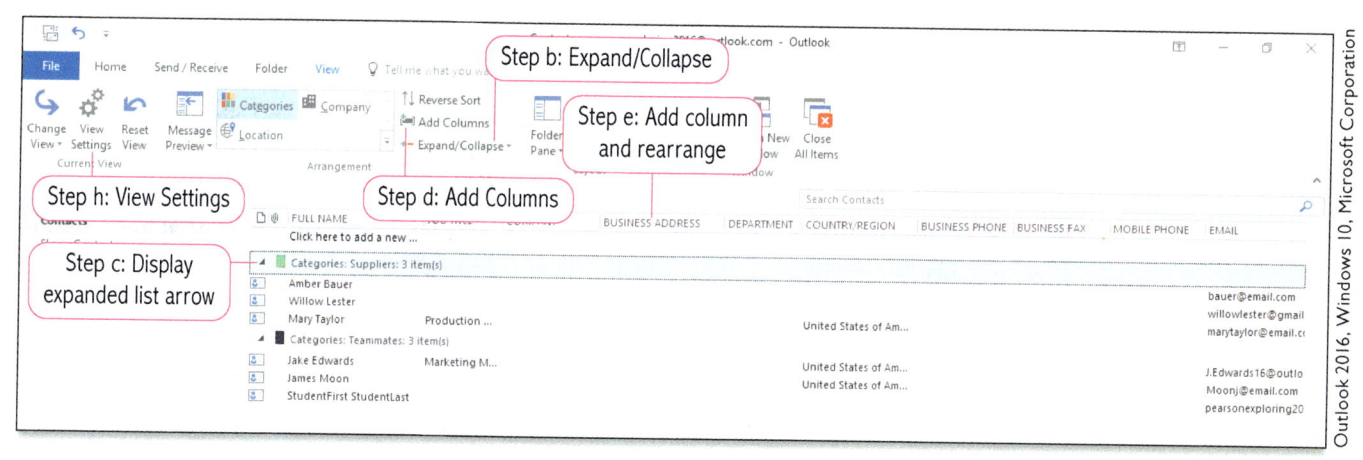

FIGURE 1.28 Organize Contacts

a. Click the **View tab**, click **Change View** in the Current View group, and then select **List**. Click **Categories** in the Arrangement group.

The entire Contacts list is displayed, showing first any contacts that are not assigned a category.

b. Click **Expand/Collapse** in the Arrangement group, and select **Collapse All Groups** so you can see the categories that you created in Step 2 but not the people.

c. Click the **display expanded list arrow** next to the categories you created in Step 2 to display the contacts within each category, as shown in Figure 1.28.

d. Click **Add Columns** in the Arrangement group.

The Show Columns dialog box displays. You may add or remove columns from the display, leaving only the columns you use regularly.

e. Click **Business Address** in the Available columns box, and click **Add** to send it to the bottom of the *Show these columns in this order* box. Click **Move Up** to move the field to position it below Company. Ensure the Department field is on the list, and position it below Business Address.

TROUBLESHOOTING: The fields can be moved up or down by dragging them. A red dashed line will indicate where the field will be placed as it is moved up or down.

f. Click the **Home Phone field** in the *Show these columns in this order* box, and click **Remove**. Click the **File As field**, and click **Remove**.

You decided not to display the home phone numbers or the File As information on this list.

Hands-On Exercise 2   39

g. Click **OK** to close the Show Fields dialog box.

This does not delete the information you may have placed in these fields on the contact records. It only makes the home phone unavailable in the list views and lists only the full name with the contact information.

> **TROUBLESHOOTING:** If you do not see the fields you added, use the scroll bar at the bottom of the window to view the columns on the right side of the Contacts list.

h. Click **View Settings** in the Current View group. Click **Filter**, and click the **More Choices tab** in the Filter dialog box. Click **Categories**, and select the **Teammates category** that you added in Step 2. Click **OK** to close the Color Categories dialog box.

i. Click **OK** to close the Filter dialog box, and click **OK** to close the Advanced View Settings: List dialog box.

You have filtered out all of the categories except the Teammates category so that you can focus on that group. The Birthday category may be visible because the classmate you set up the birthday for is in the Teammates category.

j. Click the **Home tab**, and click **New Contact Group**. Type **Teammates** in the Name box.

k. Click **Add Members** in the Members group of the window, and select **From Outlook Contacts**.

All of the contacts are displayed in the Select Members: Contacts dialog box.

l. Type in the first few letters of the name of one of your classmate contacts in the Search box. The selection bar jumps to the first occurrence that contains those characters. Double-click the name to add it to the Contact Group, or select the name, and click **Members** below the Address list.

m. Select your own name to add to the Contact Group. Add a few more contacts to the list.

n. Click **OK** to close the Select Members: Contacts dialog box.

The Contact Group window shows all of the members you selected for this group.

> **TROUBLESHOOTING:** If you select the same name more than once, Outlook will only list the person once in the Contact Group. If you decide to remove someone from the group, select the person's name, and click Remove Member in the Members group.

o. Click **Save & Close** in the Actions group to close the dialog box.

You do not see the Contact Group on your Contacts list because it has not yet been assigned a category and you are viewing the filtered list that focuses on Teammates.

p. Click the **View tab**, click **Change View**, and then select **Phone**. The Contact Group is stored in alphabetical order with the rest of your contacts in your Contacts list.

STEP 4 » USE THE CONTACT GROUP TO SEND EMAIL

You decide to send your teammates an email message to test the Contact Group. Refer to Figure 1.29 as you complete Step 4.

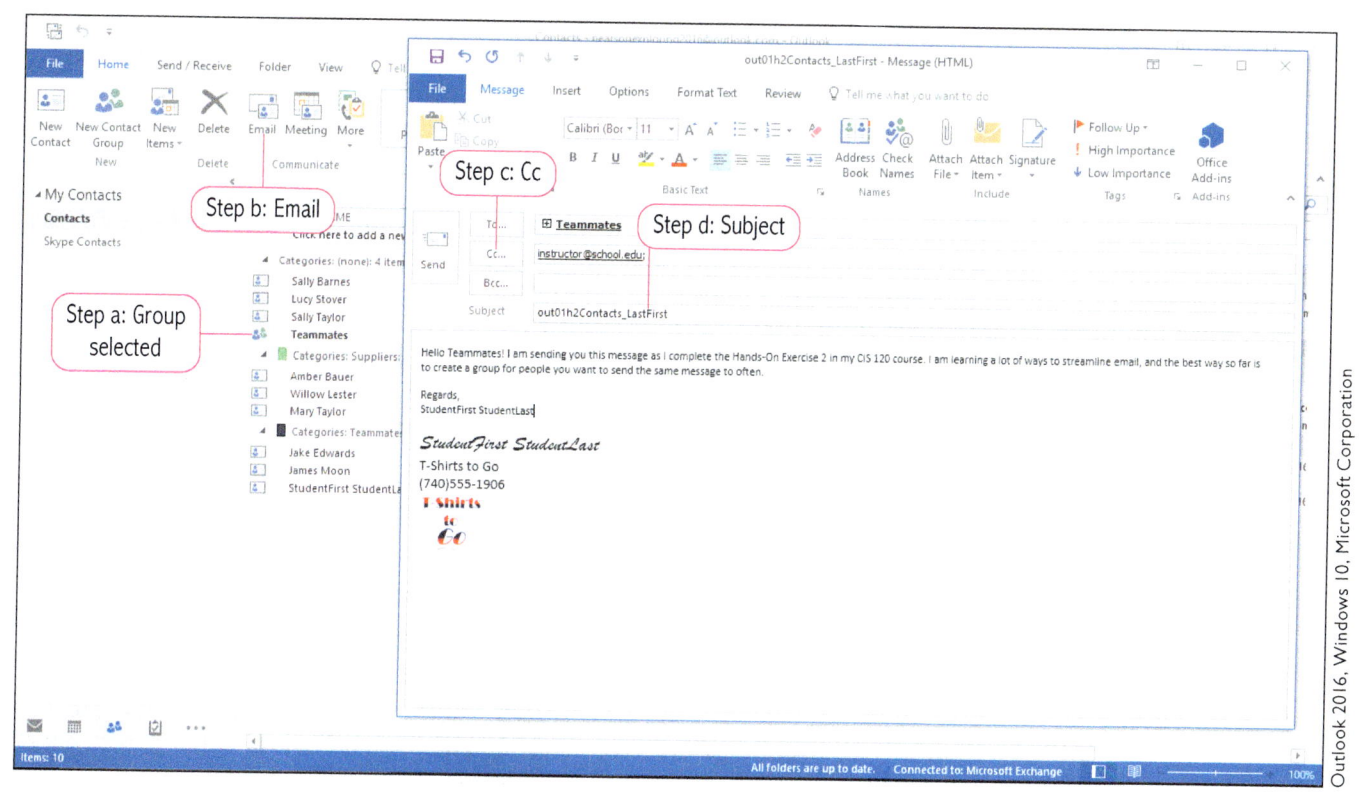

FIGURE 1.29 Send Email to a Contact Group

a. Click the **Teammates group** that you created in Step 3 to select it.

b. Click **Email** in the Communicate group on the Home tab.

c. Click **Cc**, and double-click your instructor's email address from the list of Contacts. Click **OK** to close the Select Names dialog box when you are finished.

d. Click in the **Subject box**. Type **out01h2Contacts_LastFirst** as the subject of your message, and press **Tab** once to move to the message area.

e. Type a greeting to your teammates, sure to check the spelling, proofread the message, and use professional language as you compose the greeting. Sign the message with your first and last names. Mention that you are working on completing the Hands-On Exercises so that they will not be confused about the purpose of the message. Click **Send** to send the message to everyone on the list.

f. Click the **Teammates group** in the list of contacts. Click the **File tab**, and click **Print**. Click the **Printer arrow**, and select **Microsoft Print to PDF**. Two pages appear in the preview. Click **Print**. Name the file **out01h2TeammatesContacts_LastFirst**. You will submit this file to your instructor at the end of Hands-On Exercise 3.

g. Keep Outlook open if you plan to continue with Hands-On Exercise 3. Exit Outlook if you do not want to continue with the next exercise at this time.

Hands-On Exercise 2   41

Outlook Calendar, Task List, and Notes

Busy managers will tell you that the majority of their time is spent in meetings, making and returning phone calls, and managing their schedules. Outlook enables you to organize your schedule with a calendar. Appointments added to your calendar will trigger reminders.

The Outlook Tasks list is an invaluable tool for planning your workday, week, or month. The tasks can be scheduled, categorized, marked as complete, and even assigned to other people. Reminders, follow up flagged items, and tasks appear on the To-Do List and are displayed on the To-Do Bar.

Notes, like sticky notes that you might post as a reminder, are available in Outlook. The notes can be formatted and saved. If you carry a laptop computer, you might find the Notes function to be good for taking notes during meetings.

In this section, you will look at the management functions of the calendar, setting up meetings and appointments. You will experiment with the Tasks list to plan for jobs that need to be completed. You will manage your tasks by setting reminders and categories. You will add notes to Outlook.

Managing the Outlook Calendar

The Calendar in Outlook contains a number of views so that you can select the best one for your situation. People prefer to see different views of the calendar. Some people like to see only the calendar for a day, others prefer a weekly view, and others want to see the big picture of a full month. You will probably find that you will use all three views from time to time. Figure 1.30 shows several of the calendar features in the Day view.

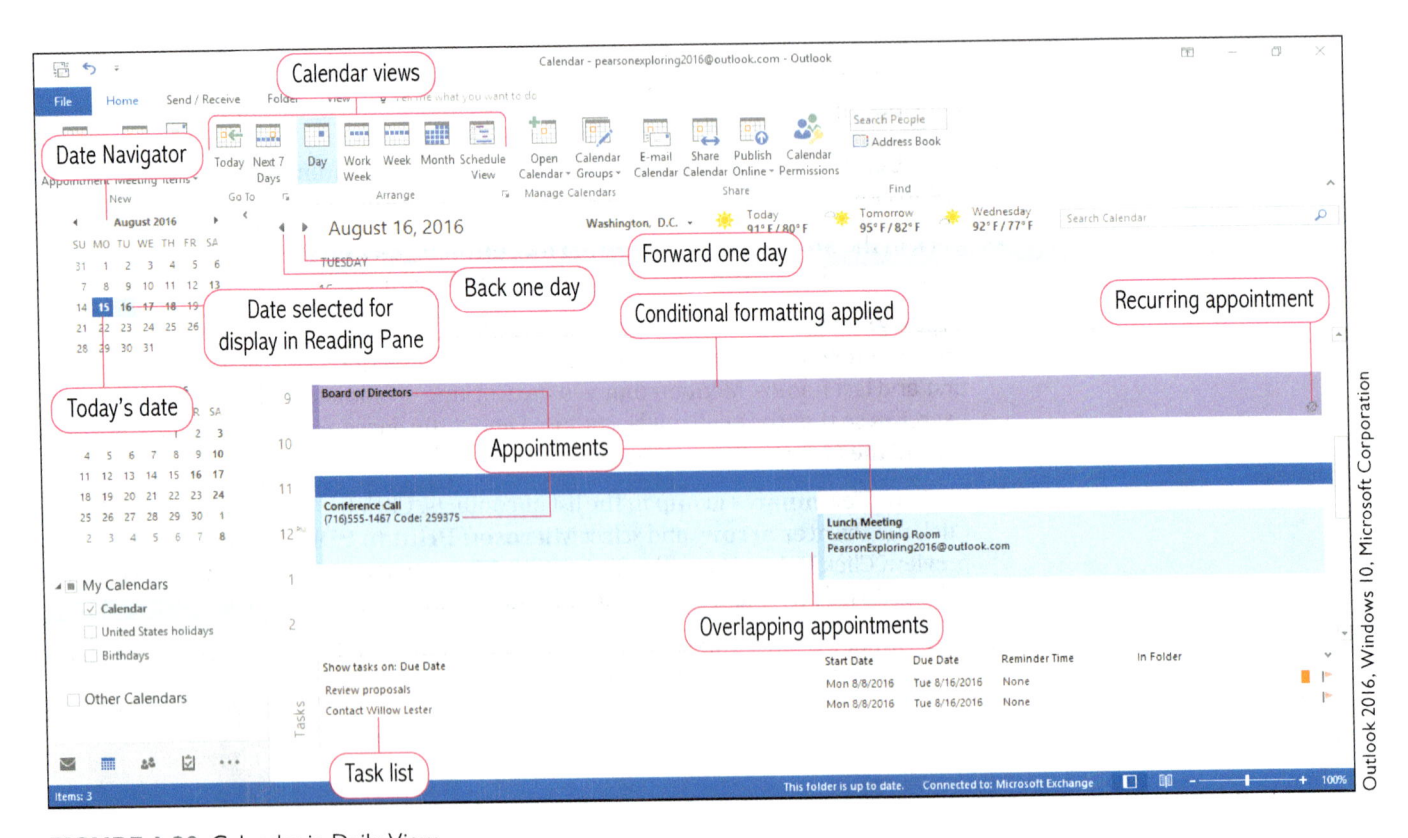

FIGURE 1.30 Calendar in Daily View

CHAPTER 1 • Managing Email, Contacts, Tasks, and Calendars

The right side of the calendar window displays the schedule for the day that is selected in the **Date Navigator**, the monthly calendar in the Folder Pane. Today's date is highlighted in dark blue on the Date Navigator. Navigate between the days by selecting a different day of the month to show the schedule for that day. The Forward and Back buttons at the top of the calendar display the next or previous day, week, or month. The Date Navigator can be widened to show more months by dragging the right edge of the Folder Pane to the right.

STEP 1 » Create Appointments and Meetings

If you need to block off a period of time on the calendar, and you do not have to schedule other people or resources, such as locations, you can create an ***appointment***. If, on the other hand, you need to schedule one or more attendees, you can create a ***meeting***. When a meeting is scheduled, Outlook will automatically create and send email notifications to the invitees.

To create an appointment, complete the following steps:

1. Open the Calendar and click New Appointment in the New Group on the Home tab.
2. Type a descriptive Subject and a Location for the appointment.
3. Select the Start and End time/date, or select All day event.
4. Type a message in the message box, and then click Save & Close to add the appointment to your calendar.

To create a meeting, complete the following steps:

1. Open the Calendar and click New Meeting in the New Group.
2. Type or select the names of the contacts you want to invite to the meeting. If you click the To button, you can specify whether the people are Required or Optional participants.
3. Type a descriptive Subject and a Location for the meeting.
4. Select the Start and End time/date, or select All day event.
5. Type a message in the message box, and then click Send to add the appointment to your calendar and send the meeting invitation to the people you specified.

> **TIP: SET UP AN APPOINTMENT FROM AN EMAIL MESSAGE**
> Email messages that contain time and date information can be used to set up calendar events. Drag the email message onto the Calendar component on the Folder Pane. The appointment window opens, enabling you to fine-tune the time and date settings. The message itself appears in the message area of the appointment window for your future reference.

Overlapping meetings or appointments are shown adjacent to one another in the same time period (refer to Figure 1.30). Outlook enables you to set up recurring events and to select the number of times the meeting or appointment recurs. It then reserves the time for all future occurrences in the series. If the Reminder option is turned on, Outlook will notify you prior to the meeting.

The schedule in Figure 1.30 shows half-hour time blocks by default. You can change the default time settings to 5-, 6-, 10-, 15-, 30-, or 60-minute increments. You can also change the workweek to start on any day, for someone who works Tuesday through Saturday, for instance. The default start time can be changed to any hour of the day to accommodate someone working on a different shift.

Use Conditional Formatting

You can apply *conditional formatting*, such as different colored shading, to appointments on your calendar to remind yourself that a meeting is important or requires preparation. Conditional formatting requires that you enter a rule that Outlook uses to apply the formatting. If you enter the name of the project as the rule, for example, any other appointments or meetings that you set up later that contain that project name will be displayed with the conditional format you selected.

To apply conditional formatting to appointments, complete the following steps:

1. Open the Calendar and select the appointment to which you want to apply conditional formatting.
2. Click the View tab, and click View Settings.
3. Click Conditional Formatting on the Advanced View Settings dialog box.
4. Click Add on the Conditional Formatting dialog box.
5. Type a name and select a color for the conditional formatting.
6. Click Condition, and type the search conditions on the Filter dialog box. Click OK to close the Filter dialog box, click OK to close the Conditional Formatting dialog box, and then click OK to close the Advanced View Settings Calendar dialog box and apply the conditional formatting to the calendar.

TIP: GETTING REMINDERS
When the Reminder option is active, each calendar entry will produce a Reminder dialog box. Click the File tab, select Options, and then click Calendar. Click the Default reminders check box to select it in the Calendar options area. Use the arrow to select the time frame for the notification prior to the entry and click OK to close the Outlook Option dialog box. Individual appointments may also contain reminders that are for less or more time than specified by the default reminder. As you create the appointment, click the Reminder arrow, and select a notification time frame.

Figure 1.31 shows the calendar in Month view with the Date Navigator minimized. This view gives you a quick idea of your schedule for the whole month. If there are too many meetings and appointments in one day to display in the monthly view, you can access a specific day's appointments and meetings by clicking the arrow within that day. Double-clicking an item on the calendar will bring up details about that appointment or meeting. To add appointments to the monthly view calendar, double-click the open space for the day and time, and an appointment dialog box displays. All-day events such as the Conference on August 15, shown in Figure 1.31, display lightly shaded for the entire day.

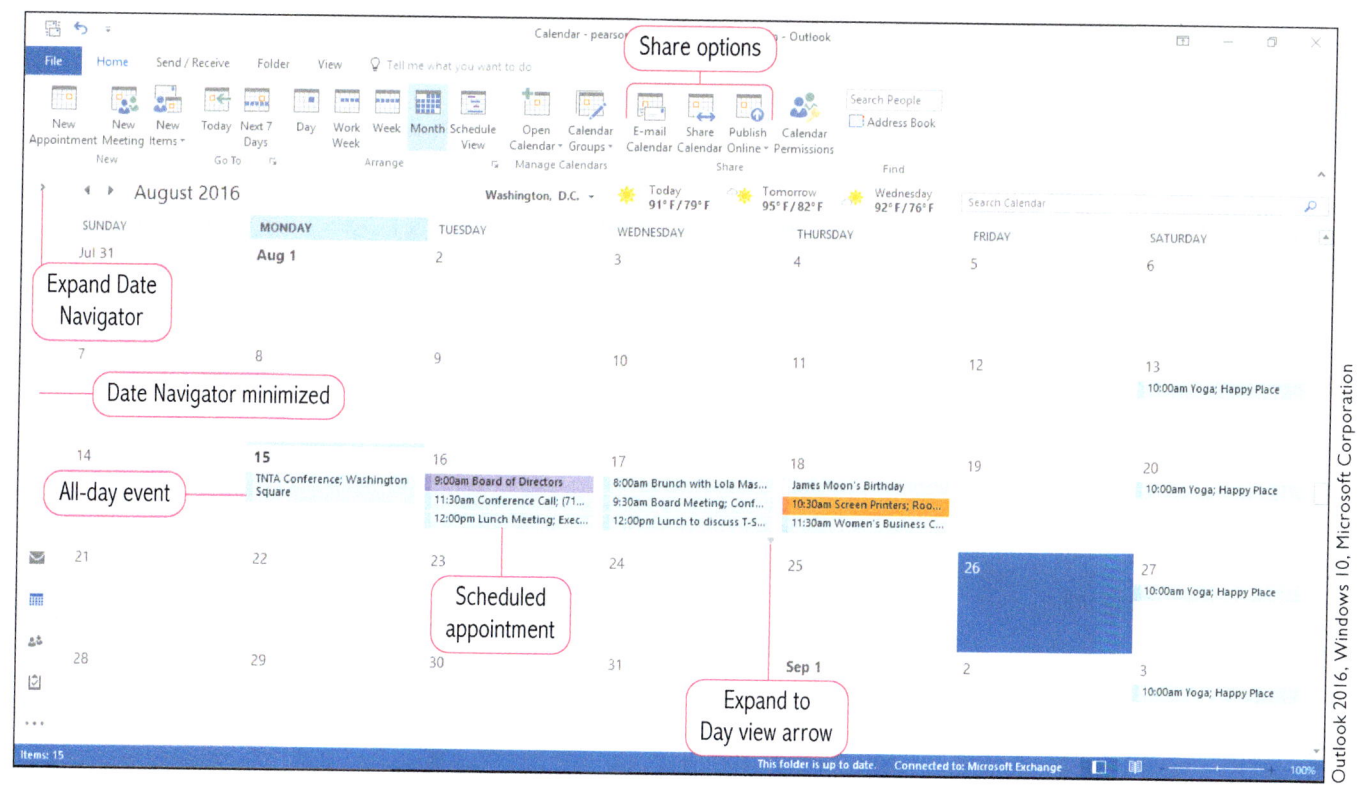

FIGURE 1.31 Calendar in Monthly View

More than one calendar can be created in Outlook. You may find it very helpful to have a personal calendar and a professional calendar (to share with others) that track your appointments, meetings, and events. Just as you created new folders in Outlook Mail, you can add new calendars to your My Calendars list. Outlook will display the calendars individually or you can view multiple calendars at one time.

Share Your Calendar

STEP 2 You can share your calendar so that people in your office will know what your planned responsibilities are for the day, week, or month. For instance, you can email your calendar to your assistant or supervisor to inform them of your travel plans and appointments. If you have a Microsoft Exchange server account, you can share your calendar and request an invitation to view other people's calendars. Calendars can also be published on a server. While viewing your calendar, click the option you want on the Share group on the Home tab and complete the entries in the dialog box. You can select settings to display Limited details, Full details, or Availability only.

Managing Tasks and Notes

STEP 3 Just as the calendar can keep you on track for appointments, the Outlook Tasks, shown in Figure 1.32, enables you to see tasks you have set, as well as a To-Do List that includes items for which you have specified a reminder. This is especially helpful if you would like to remember to follow up on an email message you received. The To-Do Bar can be displayed with a calendar, people you have set as favorites, and tasks. Click the View tab in any Outlook component, click To-Do Bar in the Layout group, and select the option you want. It is convenient to use the To-Do Bar to add new tasks quickly to your Tasks list in these other components.

Below the calendar in Figure 1.30 is the Tasks list that shows each task you have entered with an indication of its status. Only outstanding tasks for the date will be displayed. Time can be reserved for tasks by dragging and dropping any task onto the calendar. The Tasks list can be resized by clicking on the top bar of the Tasks list and dragging it up or down.

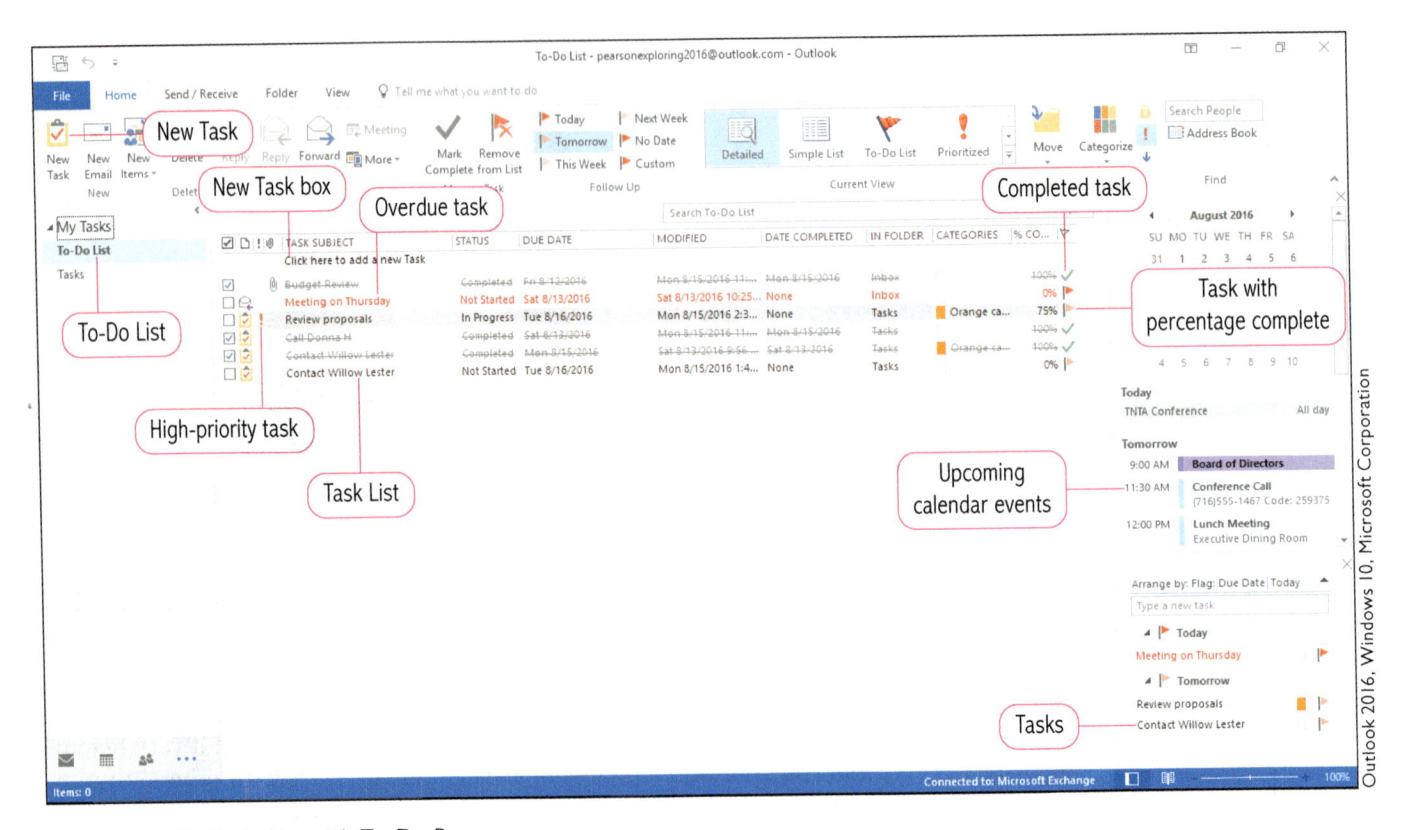

FIGURE 1.32 Tasks List with To-Do Bar

Tasks are displayed with different characteristics based on their status. Tasks marked as completed are shown with a line drawn through them. Tasks shown in red text indicate overdue tasks. The flag colors indicate the nearness of the deadline by turning from yellow to red as the due date approaches and passes. And as with just about everything else in Outlook, tasks can be categorized by color and displayed in category order.

The progress you make on tasks is also displayed in the Tasks list. Status settings include Not Started, In Progress, Completed, Waiting on someone else, and Deferred. Priority settings of Low Importance, Normal, and High Importance may be specified. You can even record the percentage of completeness of the task.

Add Tasks

You can enter new tasks by double-clicking on a blank line on the Tasks list, clicking in the New Task box, or clicking New Task in the New group on the Home tab. In the New Task box, each field (Subject, Due date) is clicked individually to add the information. Double-clicking in the New Task box or clicking New Task in the New group causes a dialog box to open, which is more convenient and displays additional options. Tasks can also be typed quickly into the To-Do Bar while using any of the other components of Outlook.

Add Notes

You may have sticky notes posted all over your desk, office, or refrigerator. Using Outlook, you can clean up your work area by using the Notes function. Notes will often contain quick little memory joggers, but you may also use this function to record meeting notes or class notes.

The Notes "pad" is available by clicking Notes at the bottom of the Folder Pane (you may have to click […] first) and clicking New Note in the New group on the Home tab. As shown in Figure 1.33, the note is yellow, and records the time and date the note was made. The note writing space can be made larger by dragging the corner of the window, just as you would resize any other window. The notes are stored as an Outlook data file. They can be viewed by clicking Notes at the bottom of the Folder Pane. Notes can also be assigned to categories that change the appearance of the note in the Reading Pane.

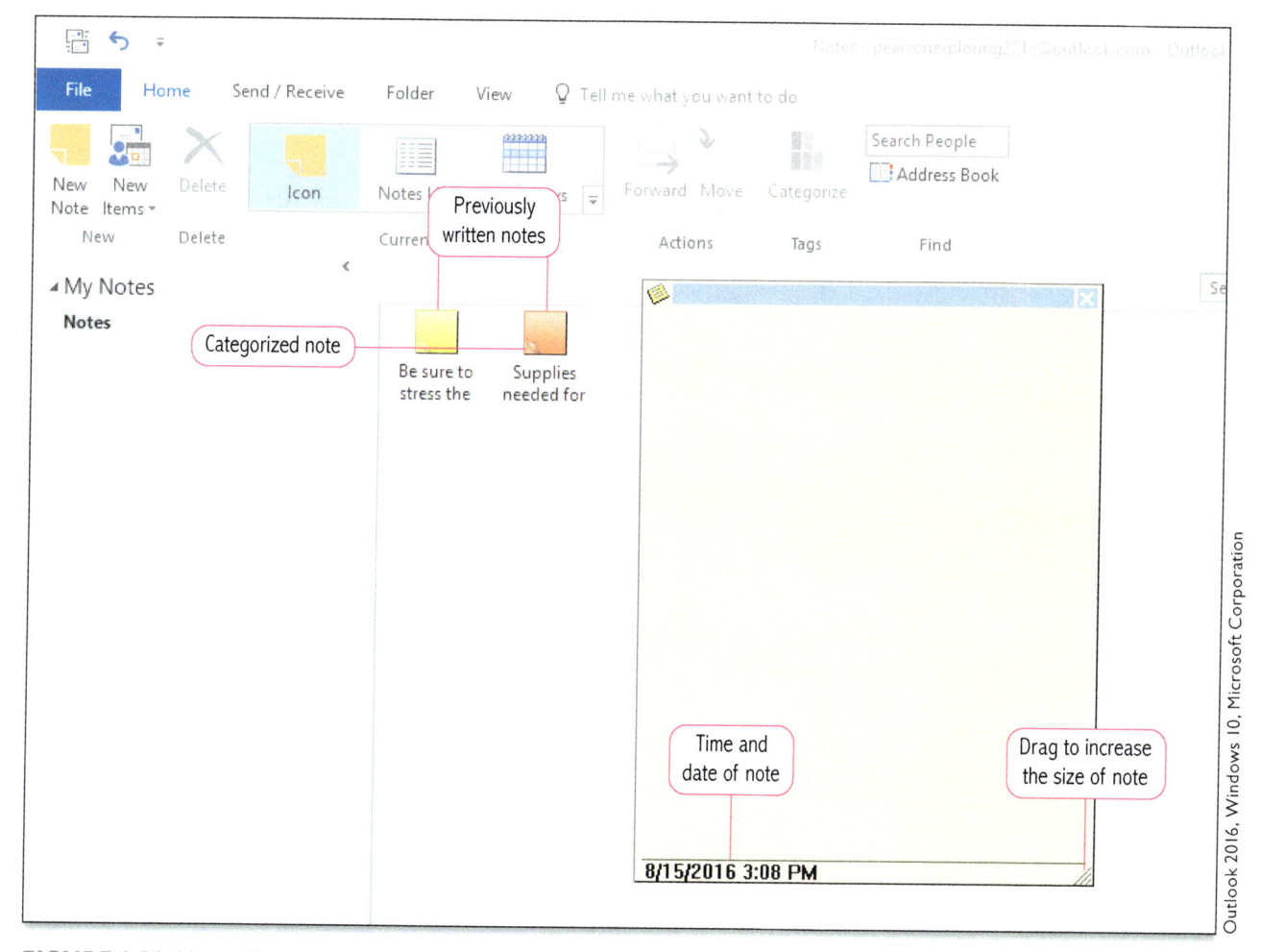

FIGURE 1.33 Notes Component

> **TIP: REMOVING ITEMS**
> If there is an entry in the calendar, contacts, email, or task list that you would like to remove, select the item and press Delete. Entries deleted in this way will move to the Deleted Items folder on the Outlook Mail Folder Pane.

Quick Concepts

6. Describe the differences in an appointment and a meeting. ***p. 43***
7. Describe the circumstances in which you would create tasks and notes. Be specific and give examples. ***p. 45, 47***

Outlook Calendar, Task List, and Notes • Outlook   47

Hands-On Exercises

Skills covered: Enter an Appointment • Add Conditional Formatting • Share a Calendar • Create a Task • Print a Task List as a PDF File • Create a Note • Print a Note as a PDF File

3 Outlook Calendar, Task List, and Notes

With all of your classes, social activities, and volunteer events, your schedule is hectic. Adding the entrepreneurship project to your busy calendar makes you realize that you really need a good way to plan your week. You want to place appointments on the calendar and add formatting to help you organize your activities. You will use Outlook to create a task list to plan for jobs that need to be completed. You will manage your tasks by setting reminders and categories. You will experiment by adding notes to Outlook.

STEP 1 » ENTER AN APPOINTMENT AND ADD CONDITIONAL FORMATTING

You will create an appointment on the Outlook calendar and add a reminder, which will appear 10 minutes before the appointment is to begin. You decide that color-coding items that relate to the entrepreneurship project is a good idea. This will cause the activities to stand out on your calendar. Refer to Figure 1.34 as you complete Step 1.

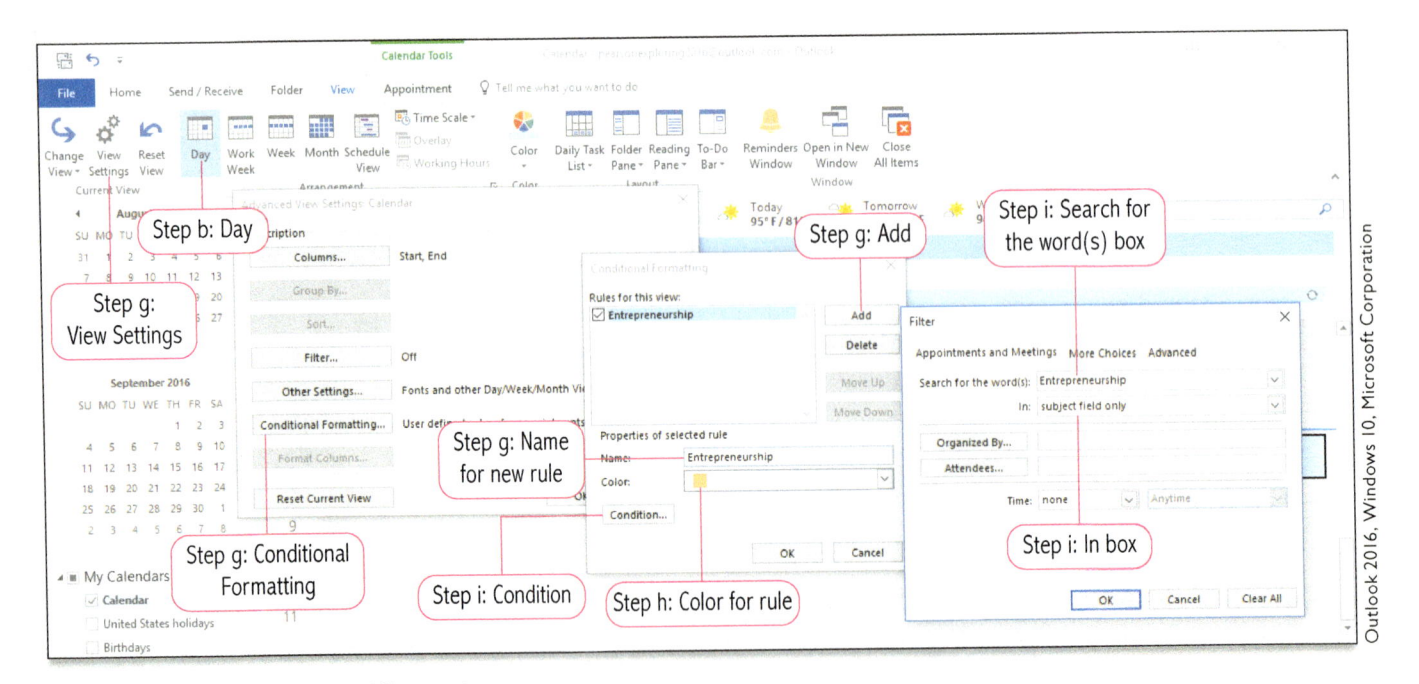

FIGURE 1.34 Add Conditional Formatting

a. Open Outlook if you closed it at the end of Hands-On Exercise 2. Click **Calendar** on the Folder Pane to display the calendar window.

b. Click **Day** in the Arrange group on the Home tab, and click **Today** in the Go To group to display today's date.

You should see your schedule for today.

c. Click **New Appointment** in the New group to open the Appointment window.

d. Type **Entrepreneurship Project Meeting** in the Subject box, and type **Room 104** in the Location box. Enter the starting time of the appointment as 10 minutes from now. Enter an ending time one hour after that.

e. Click the **Reminder arrow** in the Options group, and select **5 minutes**. (When the message pops up to remind you of this hypothetical appointment, click **Dismiss** or press **Esc** to close the Reminder dialog box, and continue working.)

f. Click **High Importance** in the Tags group. Click **Save & Close** to save the appointment.

Two priority settings, High Importance and Low Importance, signal you of the urgency of the meeting. Your appointment will appear in the daily schedule at the time you entered and the High Importance setting will be visible when you display the appointment.

g. Click the **View tab**, click **View Settings** in the Current View group, and then click **Conditional Formatting** to display the Conditional Formatting dialog box shown in Figure 1.34. Click **Add**, and type **Entrepreneurship** in the Name box as a name for this rule.

h. Click the **Color arrow** to display the possible colors. Select **Peach**.

> **TROUBLESHOOTING:** To determine the names of the colors in the palette, pause with the pointer over the color. The color name will appear as a ScreenTip.

i. Click **Condition** to display the Filter dialog box. Type **Entrepreneurship** in the *Search for the word(s) box*. Ensure the In box shows subject field only, and click **OK** to close the Filter dialog box. Click **OK** to close the Conditional Formatting dialog box. Click **OK** to close the Advanced View Settings: Calendar dialog box.

The appointment you previously scheduled in Step 1 displays with a peach-colored background.

> **TROUBLESHOOTING:** If the shading does not appear, make sure that you have typed the search word exactly as you did in the appointment you set and the entrepreneurship item check box is selected when you return to the conditions dialog box.

j. Click the **Home tab**, and select **New Appointment** in the New group. Type **Entrepreneurship Meeting** in the Subject box. Click the **Start time calendar**, and select tomorrow's date. Click the **Start time arrow** for the time, and select **1:00 PM**. Click **Save & Close** in the Actions group.

k. Click tomorrow's date in the Date Navigator to view the appointment. You may have to scroll up or down the Day view in order to find the time frame for which you set the appointment.

The appointment will display with a peach background. The search word Entrepreneurship will trigger the color-coding regardless of additional words that may appear in the subject line.

l. Click the **Home tab** and click the **Dialog Box Launcher** in the Go To group. Enter your classmate's birth date that you used in Step 2 of Hands-On Exercise 2 in the dialog box, and click **OK** to close the dialog box and display the day.

Your classmate's name is at the top of the calendar in the All-Day Event bar.

m. Click the **View tab**, click **View Settings**, and then click **Conditional Formatting**. Click **Add**, and type **Birthday** for the name for the rule. Select **Dark Red** for the color. Click **Condition**, and type **Birthday** for the search word. Click **OK** to close the Filter dialog box. Click **OK** to close the Conditional Formatting dialog box, and click **OK** to close the Advanced View Settings: Calendar dialog box.

Note that the color of the All-Day Event bar has changed. You have set conditional formatting on the birthday field and this color will be applied to any future birthdays you set up in Outlook Contacts.

STEP 2 » EMAIL A CALENDAR

You realize that your team will need to know what you are planning to do in the coming week. You will send an email to share your calendar. Refer to Figure 1.35 as you complete Step 2.

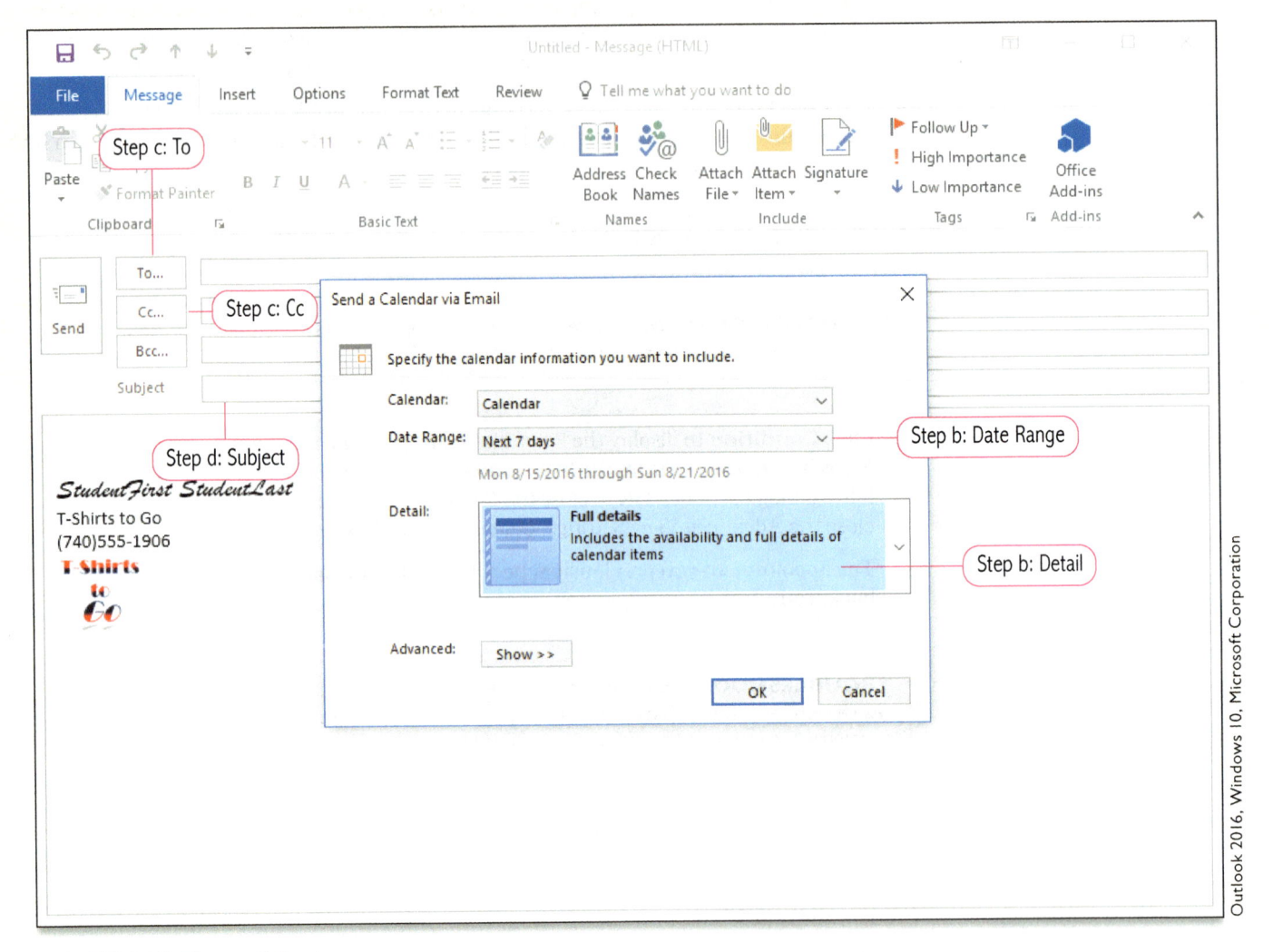

FIGURE 1.35 Share a Calendar

a. Click the **Home tab** and click **E-Mail Calendar** in the Share group. Click the **Date Range arrow** and select **Next 7 days**. Click the **Detail arrow**, and select **Full details**. Click **OK**.

You note that each style is shown in a thumbnail view and that a preview of your actual calendar is shown in the Preview pane.

b. Double-click **To** and double-click **your instructor's name**. Click **OK**. Type **your email address** in the Cc box.

c. Change the Subject to **out01h3Calendar_LastFirst**.

d. Review the calendar in the Reading Pane, and click **Send**. Evaluate each spelling error that is displayed and click Ignore or Change as appropriate.

CHAPTER 1 • Hands-On Exercise 3

STEP 3 » CREATE A TASK

You will create tasks and manipulate the settings for those tasks to experiment with this component of Outlook. You decide to experiment with Outlook Notes. Refer to Figure 1.36 as you complete Step 3.

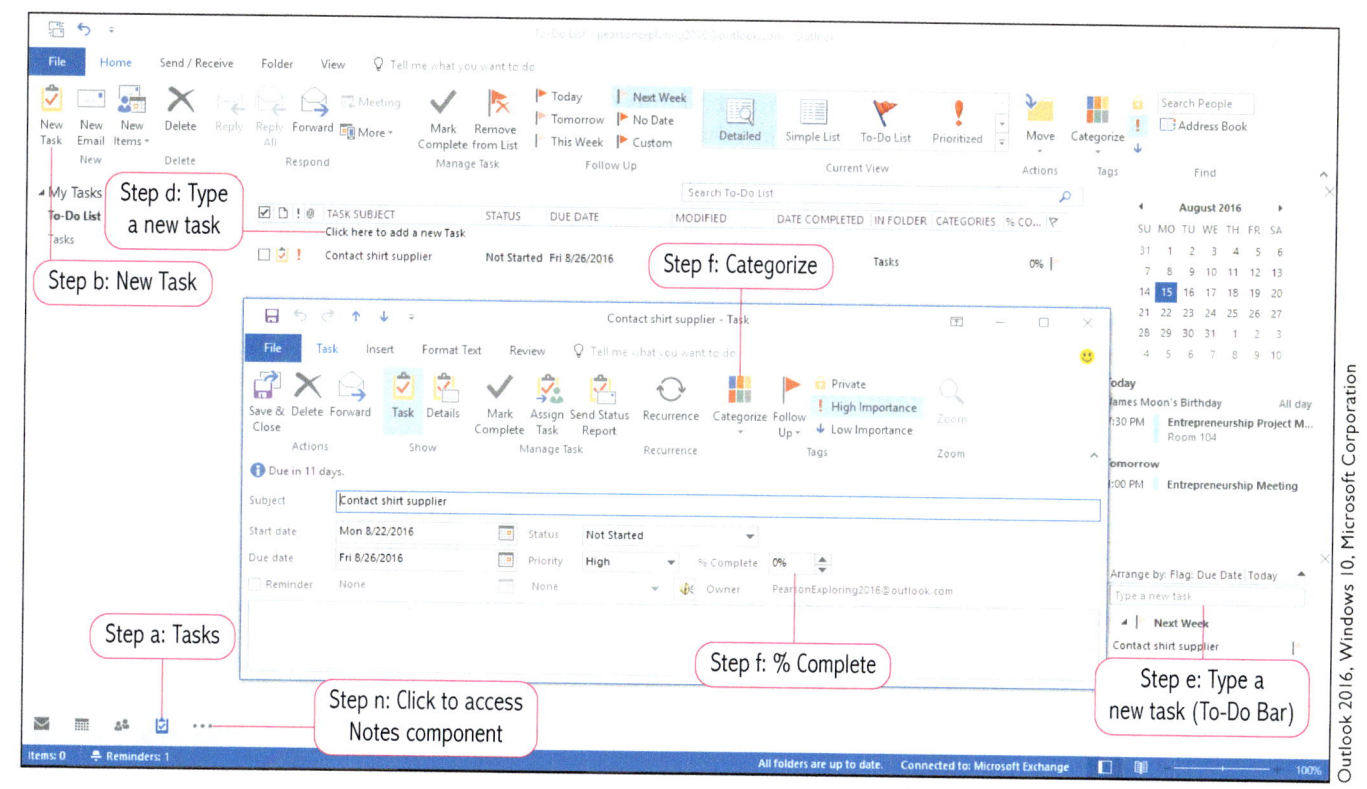

FIGURE 1.36 Create a Task

a. Click **Tasks** on the Folder Pane to display the Tasks window.

b. Click **New Task** in the New group on the Home tab to see the Task window shown in Figure 1.36.

c. Type the Subject **Contact shirt supplier**. Select a Start date of next Monday and a Due date of next Friday. Set the Priority to **High Importance**. Click **Save & Close** in the Actions group to create the first task.

d. Click in the **Type a new task box** at the top of the Tasks work area, and type **Call Screen Printer**. Press **Enter** to add the task to the task list.

e. Ensure that the insertion point is in the Type a new task box in the To-Do Bar, and type **Develop Logo**. Press **Enter**.

> **TROUBLESHOOTING:** If you do not see the To-Do Bar, click the View tab, click To-Do Bar in the Layout group, and then click Tasks.

f. Double-click in the space below the task list to open a dialog box and create another task. Type **Prepare presentation for advisor** in the Subject box. Select a Start date of next Monday and a Due date of next Friday. Change % Complete to **50**. Click **Categorize** in the Tags group, and select the **Teammates category**. Click **Save & Close**.

> **TROUBLESHOOTING:** If you cannot set the category because you are using an IMAP account, just save and close the task without assigning a category.

Hands-On Exercise 3   51

g. Point to the **Call screen printer task** in the To-Do Bar and drag it below the Develop Logo task.

You can drag items to set your priorities for your tasks in the To-Do Bar. The red line indicates the position of the item you are dragging.

h. Click **Calendar** in the Folder Pane. Ensure the To-Do Bar is displayed (click the View tab, click To-Do Bar in the Layout group, and select Tasks).

i. Click the **Type a new task box** on the To-Do Bar, type **Create Printing Budget**, and press **Enter**. Confirm that the task has been set.

j. Click **Tasks** at the bottom of the Folder Pane, to return to the Tasks component.

k. Click the first task on the Task list, press and hold **Shift**, and then click the second task.

l. Click the **File tab**, and select **Print** to display Print Settings. Click **Table Style** to select it.

m. Click **Print Options** to display the Print dialog box. Click **Only selected rows**. Click **Preview** to see what will be printed. Click the **Printer arrow** and select **Microsoft Print to PDF**. Click **Print**.

n. Navigate to the location where you store your files, and type **out01h3Tasks_LastFirst** as a file name. Click **Save**.

o. Click [⋯] at the bottom of the Folder Pane and click **Notes** to show the Icon Notes view.

> **TROUBLESHOOTING:** If you do not see the Icon Notes view, click Icon in the Current View group of the Home tab.

p. Click the **View tab**, and click **Large Icons** in the Arrangement group.

q. Click the **Home tab**, and click **New Note** in the New group. Type the following on the sticky note, pressing **Enter** after each sentence:

Ideas for Presentation:

Bring logos in extra large format.

Print one or two sample T-shirts to give as prizes.

Survey other students to see how many of them would purchase a T-shirt.

Create charts for the PowerPoint presentation.

r. Click the **Note icon** at the top left of the sticky note, and select **Save & Close** from the shortcut menu. The note will be saved and shown in the Notes list.

s. Click **Categorize**, and click **Teammates** from the category list.

> **TROUBLESHOOTING:** If you cannot categorize the note due to working with an IMAP account, skip to the next step.

t. Ensure the note you just wrote is selected, click the **File tab**, and then click **Print**. Click the **Printer arrow** and select **Microsoft Print to PDF**. Click **Print**. Name the file **out01h3Note_LastFirst** and click **Save**.

u. Exit Outlook. Based on your instructor's directions, submit:

out01h1TeamFolder_LastFirst

out01h2TeammatesContacts_LastFirst

out01h3Tasks_LastFirst

out01h3Note_LastFirst

Chapter Objectives Review

After reading this chapter, you have accomplished the following objectives:

1. **Identify the components of the Outlook window.**
   - Microsoft Outlook is a desktop information manager that you can use to send and receive email, maintain a contact list, schedule meetings and appointments, create and track tasks, and write notes to yourself.
   - View mail: The Mail component features an Inbox on the Folder Pane with incoming email messages and a Reading Pane where you view the messages.
   - View appointments with the Calendar: The Calendar component can be displayed by day, week, or month, and enables you to keep multiple calendars.
   - View contacts: The Contacts component manages the information you have about people with whom you communicate. The information can be displayed as Business Cards, Cards, People, Phone List, or List.
   - View tasks: The Task component enables you to set and track tasks. A current task list can be displayed on the To-Do bar in other Outlook components.
   - Get help with Outlook: The *Tell me what you want to do* box enables you to find answers to your questions in how to use Outlook.

2. **Manage Email.**
   - Outlook Mail enables you to compose and manage email. The Outlook Mail client is used to upload email onto a mail server, where it is transferred to the Internet and sent to the addressed recipients. Outlook is also used to download email that has been sent to you and deliver it to your Outlook Inbox.
   - Manage the inbox: The Inbox displays the messages that have been sent to you. Messages can be arranged in the message list in the order in which they arrived, as a filtered list, or in conversations. Quick Steps enable you to perform multiple steps with a single click.
   - Create an email message: The Ribbon contains tabs and commands to enable you to compose an email message.
   - Select the recipients for your message: The To, Cc, and Bcc boxes are used for addressing the message to the recipients.
   - Compose the message: The message can include text, graphics, hyperlinks, attachments, stationery, and a signature.
   - Reply to or forward an email message: You can reply to email messages, sending your reply back to the original sender, or you can reply to everyone who received the message, or forward the message to another person.
   - Attach files: An attached file is created in another software application, and appended to the email message for transfer to the recipient.
   - Add a signature: Signatures can be appended to email messages to save you time and identify you to the recipient of the message.
   - Manage mail folders: Folders enable you to store and manage the email you generate. You can flag messages for follow up, delete messages, or move them into other folders.
   - Mark email for follow up: Messages you have flagged for follow up appear as a task on the To-Do Bar.

3. **Manage Contacts.**
   - Contact information is stored in Outlook. The information can be as simple as the name and email address of a person. It can also be robust, enabling you to record business, home, fax and mobile phone numbers, birthdays and anniversaries, and multiple addresses. Notes and photographs can be added to the contact information.
   - Change views: You can display your contacts in various ways to enable you to select the person you want to communicate with more efficiently.
   - Organize contacts: Categories organize your contacts, making it easier to find contact information for people in the same categories. You select names and colors for each category that you use. After adding contacts to Outlook, color-coded categories can be assigned to the contacts.
   - Use contacts: Once established, you can use your contacts as email message recipients, or communicate with them in other ways, such as by phone, or calendar invitations.

4. **Manage the Outlook Calendar.**
   - Although Outlook is best known for its email functions, it also is a desktop organizer that enables you to schedule your day onto a calendar. Daily, weekly, and monthly views of the calendar are available and you can print the views.
   - Create appointments and meetings: An appointment is a period of time blocked off on your calendar. A meeting enables you to schedule attendees and resources, such as rooms.
   - Use conditional formatting: Conditional formatting enables to you organize your calendar with different colored shading based on rules that you set up.
   - Share your calendar: You can share your calendar with other people so that they are aware of your planned activities, and so that they can schedule appointments and meetings that do not conflict with other activities on your calendar.

5. **Manage Task and Notes.**
    - The Outlook Tasks list helps you organize your jobs, enabling you to assign priorities to the entries, report progress, and mark them as complete. Tasks can be assigned due dates and reminders.
    - Add tasks: Tasks can be added to your task list in the New Task box, by clicking New Task on the Home tab, or typed directly on the To-Do Bar in other Outlook components. Calendar items, contacts, and email can be dragged onto the To-Do Bar task list to set up a task quickly for the item.
    - Add notes: You can create digital sticky notes using Outlook. The short notes do not have time or date restrictions on them. They are typed quickly and serve to remind you of things.

Key Terms Matching

a. Appointment
b. Attached file
c. Category
d. Conditional formatting
e. Conversation
f. Date Navigator
g. Deleted Items folder
h. Drafts folder
i. Folder Pane
j. Inbox
k. Junk Email folder
l. Meeting
m. Netiquette
n. Outbox folder
o. Quick Step
p. Reading Pane
q. Rules
r. Sent Items folder
s. To-Do Bar

1. _____ A pane on the Outlook window that contains folders, calendars, and buttons for organizing information for each of the components of Outlook. p. 5

2. _____ A default folder that receives incoming email. p. 6

3. _____ The portion of the Outlook window that displays the text of a selected message, appointment, contact, or task. p. 6

4. _____ A pane on the right side of the Outlook window that provides a quick overview of the calendar, upcoming appointments, and tasks. p. 8

5. _____ A method of automatically managing email by applying steps based on criteria as a message is received. p. 18

6. _____ A group of messages that share the same subject line and appear together with graphics indicating the relationship between the messages. p. 11

7. _____ A recycle bin that contains email that you have deleted. p. 12

8. _____ Multiple commands compressed into a single click accessed from the Ribbon email component of Outlook. p. 18

9. _____ A folder that contains all of the messages you have written that have not yet been uploaded to the server. p. 17

10. _____ A folder that contains copies of messages that have been uploaded to the mail server. p. 17

11. _____ A folder that stores email that has been saved but not sent. p. 17

12. _____ A folder that contains messages identified as possible spam by the Junk Email Filter. p. 17

13. _____ Etiquette rules for the Internet and a group of commonly accepted good practices. p. 14

14. _____ A file created in a software application that is appended to an email message for transmission to the recipient. p. 16

15. _____ An organizational feature that enables you to color-code and name groups of email, appointments, contacts, or tasks for easy retrieval. p. 32

16. _____ A monthly calendar, shown in the Folder Pane, that can be used to select a date for display on the calendar. p. 43

17. _____ An assignment of time where other people or resources are not scheduled. p. 43

18. _____ An event scheduled with one or more attendees for whom Outlook will automatically create and send email notifications. p. 43

19. _____ A process of setting up rules applied to appointments, contacts, or tasks to make them stand out from other items. p. 44

Multiple Choice

1. Your best friend is having a birthday. The easiest way to invite people to the surprise party you are planning is to:
   (a) Send each person an email invitation.
   (b) Use your contacts to create a Contact group and send one email invitation to everyone with an attachment of a map to the party location.
   (c) Add the party to your calendar in Outlook.
   (d) Create an invitation in Word, print the document, and hand it out to people as you see them during the course of the day.

2. RSVP email messages for the surprise party have been flowing into your Inbox. You would like to keep track of who is coming and who has declined. What is the best way to accomplish this using Outlook?
   (a) Create a note and type everyone's name on the note as you receive the RSVP.
   (b) Create a task and note everyone who will attend as you receive the RSVP.
   (c) Assign categories to attend or not attend, and categorize the email messages as you read them.
   (d) Make an entry on the calendar when each response is received.

3. Someone who will not be attending the party wanted to send a special note to your friend, but not spoil the surprise of the party. He attached his note as a Word document to his RSVP email message. How can you identify a message with an attachment?
   (a) An exclamation point appears next to the message in the Inbox.
   (b) The message is displayed in green.
   (c) A paperclip icon shown next to the message in the Inbox.
   (d) The message by default goes into a category for email with attachments in Outlook. Just click the category name to see the message.

4. Party plans seem to be getting out of hand. You have lots of paper reminders of things that need to be accomplished before the party. Which component of Outlook would be the best to use to organize all of these jobs?
   (a) Calendar
   (b) Email
   (c) Tasks
   (d) Contacts

5. As you look at Outlook, how can you identify tasks that are overdue for completion?
   (a) The task contains an exclamation point.
   (b) The task is shown in red text.
   (c) The task is lined through.
   (d) The task is in flashing text.

6. As a Customer Service representative, you receive an email message from a person who has a question that you cannot answer. Knowing that providing the correct answer as quickly as possible is a quality of good customer service, you:
   (a) Forward the message to the person in charge of the department that handles these types of questions using your contact email list.
   (b) Assign the message a high-priority category and assign it as a task to a co-worker.
   (c) Create a note to remind yourself to ask someone about the question.
   (d) Send the customer a reply message.

7. Which of the following would be used to organize a client list so the contacts are organized by location?
   (a) Conversations
   (b) Categories
   (c) Quick Steps
   (d) Rules

8. Timed reminders, where you receive an audible signal and see a pop-up box, can be set for:
   (a) Contacts only.
   (b) Calendar items only.
   (c) Tasks only.
   (d) Calendar items, and tasks.

9. The Calendar in Outlook:
   (a) Prevents you from setting appointments that are at the same time, keeping you from having conflicts.
   (b) Can contain only one calendar, the one set up when Outlook was installed.
   (c) Can display a task list when in the Day, Work Week, or Week view.
   (d) Has four settings for priority.

10. Meetings:
    (a) Are events to which one or more people are invited.
    (b) Cannot be assigned a category.
    (c) Appear only on the To-Do List.
    (d) Are set up using Tasks.

Practice Exercises

1 Lynch, Lynch, and Boggs Email Reminders

As a paralegal assistant for Lynch, Lynch, and Boggs, you contact clients on a daily basis to remind them of appointments and court dates. Luckily, every client provides the attorney handling his or her case with an email address. Figure 1.37 shows a sample email message you will send. You will create a folder and file messages for Bill Lynch, your supervisor, as well as for Kathleen Lynch and Margaret Boggs. You will reply to a message, forward a message, attach a file to a message, and flag a message for follow-up. Refer to Figure 1.37 as you complete this exercise.

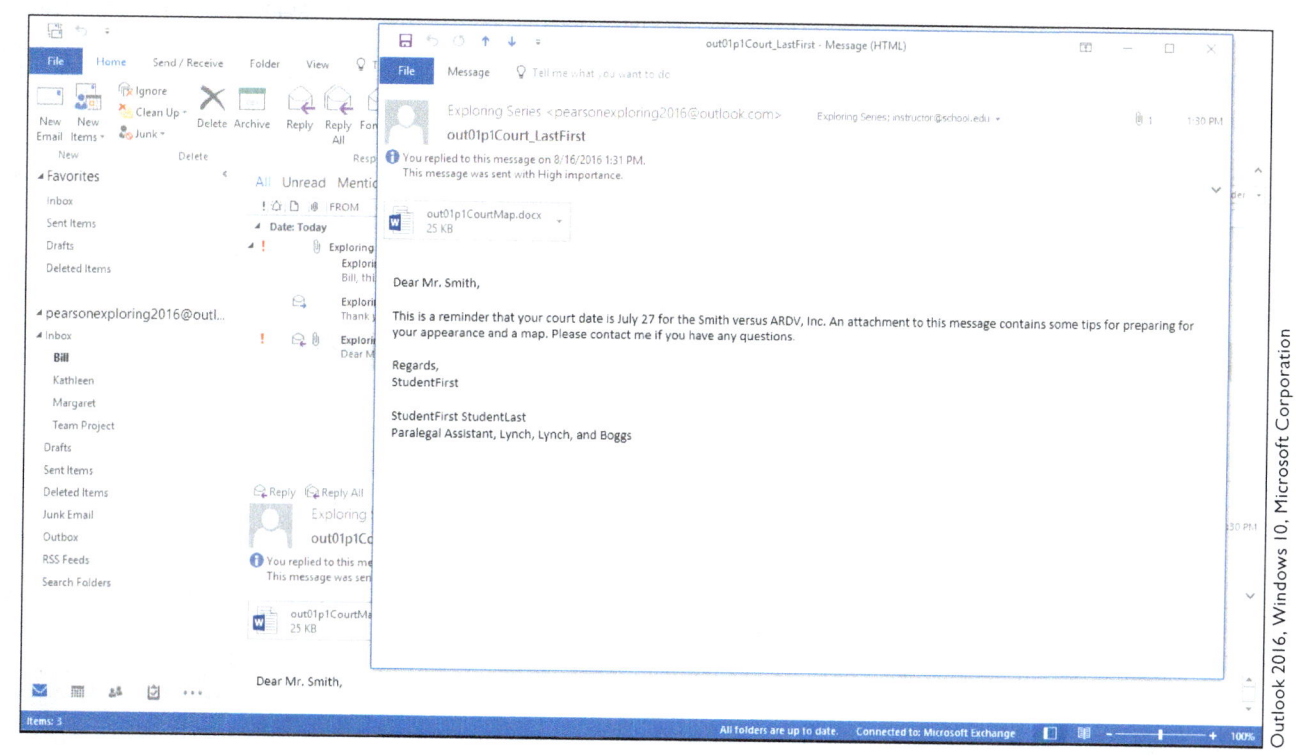

FIGURE 1.37 Email Message and Folders

a. Start Outlook, and ensure that Mail is displayed.

b. Click **New Email**. Type the email address of the recipient (your own email address) in the **To box**. Type your instructor's email address in the **Cc box**. Type a subject of **out01p1Court_ LastFirst**. Change the priority of the message to **High Importance**.

c. Enter the text of the message in the message area, as shown in Figure 1.37. Carefully proofread the message.

d. Click **Attach File** in the Include group, and click **Browse This PC** at the bottom of the list. Navigate to and select the file named *out01p1CourtMap*. Click **Insert**.

e. Click **Signature** in the Include group, and click **Signatures**. Click **New**, type **Paralegal**, and then click **OK**. Type your name in the signature box, and on the next line type **Paralegal Assistant, Lynch, Lynch, and Boggs**. Click **OK**. Click **Signature**, and select **Paralegal**.

f. Click **Send**, and click **Send/Receive All Folders** on the Quick Access Toolbar.

g. Wait a minute or two, and click **Send/Receive All Folders** to retrieve your mail from the mail server. Double-click the message in the Inbox that you just sent yourself. Click the attachment to view it in the Reading Pane.

h. Click **Reply** in the Respond group. Reply to this message, typing the following into the message area: **Thank you for the reminder of my court date. I will be there 15 minutes early and meet with Bill in the lobby.** Click **Send**.

i. Click **Send/Receive All Folders** in the Send & Receive group on the Send/Receive tab to retrieve your email from the mail server.

j. Click the most recent message you sent in your Inbox to select it. Click **Forward** in the Respond group. Type your instructor's email address in the **To box**. Add the following text to the message area: **Bill, this client has been notified of the upcoming court date**. Type your email address in the **Bcc box**. Click **Send** to send the message.

k. Click **Send/Receive All Folders** in the Send & Receive group on the Send/Receive tab to send the message. Wait a few moments, and click **Send/Receive All Folders** again to retrieve the message from the mail server.

l. Ensure the Inbox is selected, click the **Folder tab**, and then click **New Folder**. Type **Bill** in the Name box. Select the **Inbox** in the *Select where to place the folder* box. Click **OK**. Click **New Folder**, and type **Kathleen** in the Name box. Confirm that the Inbox is selected. Click **OK**. Click **New Folder**, and type **Margaret** in the Name box. Confirm that the Inbox is selected. Click **OK**.

m. Move all of the email messages you received as a result of this assignment into Bill's folder.

n. Click **Bill's folder** on the Folder Pane. Click the **View tab**. Click the **Show as Conversations box** to select it. Click **This folder** in the dialog box that displays. Click the **Expand icon** to view the messages in the conversation. Click the forwarded message in Bill's folder, and click **Follow Up** in the Tags group on the Home tab. Click **Tomorrow**.

o. Open the Snipping Tool, and take a New snip of the screen, showing the folders, and the messages. Save the snip as **out01p1Folders_LastFirst**.

p. Exit Outlook. Based on your instructor's directions, submit out01p1Folders_LastFirst.

2 Lindenville University Advisor Calendars

Part of your responsibilities as the assistant to the dean of business is to keep a schedule for all academic advisors in the office. At the beginning of each week, you print a weekly calendar for the dean so she is aware of each person's schedule. You use conditional formatting to display the entries in each advisor's color category. The advisor's first name in the subject line triggers the conditional formatting. Refer to Figure 1.38 as you complete this exercise.

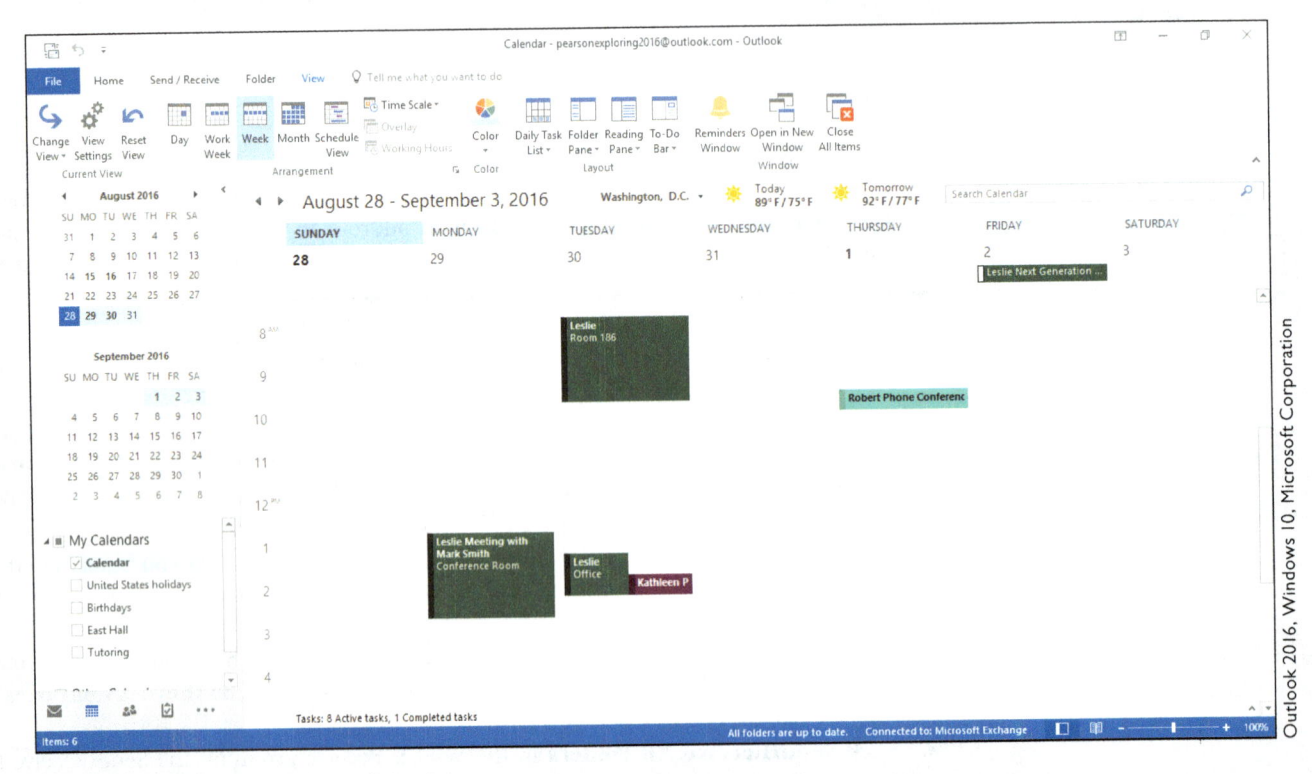

FIGURE 1.38 Advisor Weekly Calendar

a. Start Outlook. Click **Calendar** on the Folder Pane, and click the **Week** in the Arrange group. Ensure today's date is displayed in the calendar.
b. Scroll to view the 1:00 PM time frame. Double-click **1:00 PM** for next Monday. Make the new appointment, as shown in Figure 1.38, by performing the following steps:
   - Click the **Subject box**, and type **Leslie Meeting with Mark Smith**.
   - Click in the **Location box**, and type **Conference Room**.
   - Click the **End time arrow**, and click **3:00 PM**.
   - Click the **Reminder arrow**, and click **2 hours**.
   - Click in the message area, and type **Mark Smith, Interested in Paralegal program**. Save and close the appointment.
   Other appointments or tasks from the Hands-On Exercises may be visible. You can ignore those appointments and tasks.
c. Create the following appointments, using the directions in Step b.

Date	Time/Duration, Reminder	Subject	Location	Message
Next Tuesday	2:00 PM, 30 minutes	Kathleen Phone Conference	Office	Nancy Williams, 1st year advising
Next Tuesday	8:00 AM, 2 hours, Reminder 11 hours prior	Leslie	Room 186	Meet with students who have outstanding GPAs
Next Tuesday	1:30 PM, 1 hour	Leslie	Office	Amber Bauer, Undecided
Next Thursday	9:45 AM, 30 minutes, Reminder 1 hour prior	Robert Phone Conference with Council Member	Office	Mark James, Accountant Advisory Council
Next Friday	All-Day Event, Reminder 1 day	Leslie Next Generation Seminar	Conference Center	

d. Click the **View tab**, and click **View Settings** in the Current View group.
e. Click **Conditional Formatting**, click **Add**, and then type **Leslie** as a name for the rule.
f. Click **Condition**, and type **Leslie** in the *Search for the word(s)* box. Click **OK** to accept the settings in the Filter dialog box. Click the **Color arrow**, and change the color to **Dark Green**.
g. Use the Conditional Formatting dialog box to set up conditional formatting for Kathleen's appointments as **Maroon** and Robert's appointments to **Teal**. Click **OK** to close the Conditional Formatting dialog box, and click **OK** to close the Advanced View Settings dialog box.
h. Click the **File tab**, and click **Print**. Click the **Calendar Details Style** under Settings, and preview the layout. Click the **Printer arrow**, and select **Microsoft Print to PDF**. Click **Print**, name the file **out01p2Appointments_LastFirst**, and then click **Save**.
i. Exit Outlook. Based on your instructor's directions, submit out01p2Appointments_LastFirst.

3 Key Pop Promotions

As the promoter of a campus band, you are constantly juggling jobs that need to be completed on a strict timetable. You create a Task List to keep on track. You also create Notes as needed to supplement your scheduled tasks. Refer to Figure 1.39 as you complete this exercise.

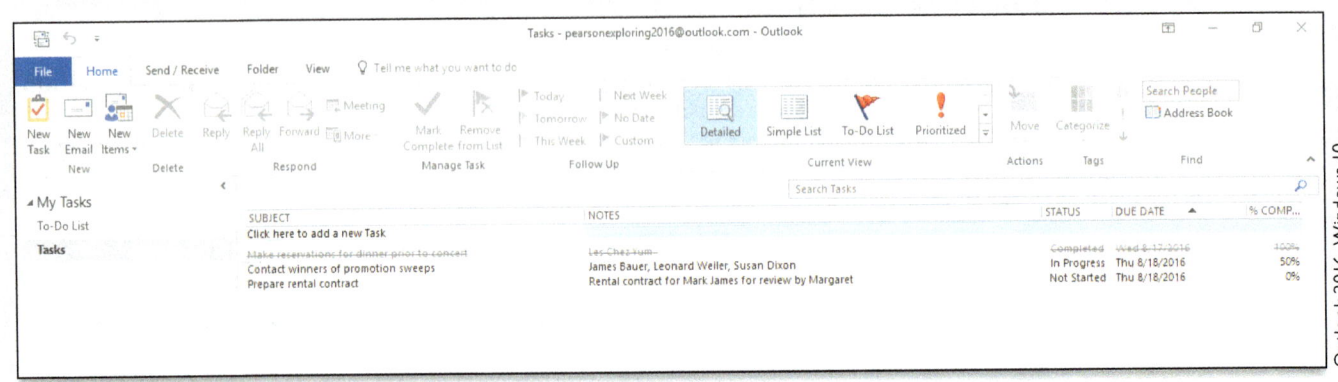

FIGURE 1.39 Outlook Tasks

a. Start Outlook. Click **Tasks** on the Folder Pane. Remove tasks that relate to the Hands-On Exercises you completed by selecting them, and clicking **Remove from List** in the Manage Task group on the Home tab.

b. Click **New Task**, and type the following task:
   - Click the **Subject box**, and type **Prepare rental contract**.
   - Click the **Start date calendar**, and select today's date.
   - Click the **Due date calendar**, and select next Thursday's date.
   - Click the **Reminder check box**, click the **Reminder date calendar**, and then select next Wednesday's date. Click the **Reminder time arrow**, and select **8:00 AM**.
   - Click in the task body, and type **Rental contract for Mark James for review by Margaret**.
   - Click **Save & Close**.

c. Continue setting tasks, as shown in the table below (make all start dates today):

Date Due	Subject	Reminder	Task Body
Next Tuesday	Arrange for radio interview	none	Everyone in band should be there. Prepare hot point notes for them to refer to during interview.
Next Wednesday	Take promo flyers to area bars, restaurants, and stores	8:00 AM, Next Tuesday	Ask permission to post a copy and leave additional copies.
Next Wednesday	Make reservations for dinner prior to concert	1:00 PM, Next Wednesday	Les Chez Yum
Next Thursday	Contact winners of promotion sweeps	none	James Bauer, Leonard Weiler, Susan Dixon

60 CHAPTER 1 • Practice Exercises

d. Click the **Make reservations task** in the Task List, and click **Mark Complete** in the Manage Task group. Double-click **Contact winners** in the Task List, and change the **% Complete** to **50%**. Click **Save & Close**.

e. Ensure that Tasks is selected in the Folder Pane. Click the **View tab**, and click **Change View** in the Current View group. Click **Detailed**. Click **View Settings** in the Current View group, and click **Columns**. Select column names, and click **Add and Remove** until only the Subject, Notes, Status, Due Date, and % Complete columns are listed in the *Show these columns in this order* box. Click **OK**. Click **OK** to close the Advanced View Settings: To Do List dialog box.

f. Click the **File tab**, and click **Print**. Click the **Printer arrow**, and select **Microsoft Print to PDF**. Click **Print**, name the file **out01p3TasksList_LastFirst**, and then click **Save**.

g. Click the **Notes icon** in the Folder Pane. Remove notes from the Hands-On Exercises you completed by selecting them, and clicking **Delete**. Click **New Note** in the New group of the Home tab, and type **Margaret wants to eat at the Warehouse or at the Lobster Trap for the meeting with Wade Cooper.**

h. Click **New Note**, and type the playlist for the upcoming concert for the band: **Prepaid and Sad, Documents of a Lost Love, Key Proposals, Journey into Inner Space, Hot and Cool, United Evidence, Blonde Waves, Uptown Swirls, Full Moon.**

i. Click **Notes List** in the Current View group. Click the **File tab**, and click **Print**. Click **Table Style**. Click the **Printer arrow**, and select **Microsoft Print to PDF**. Click **Print**, name the file **out01p3NotesList_LastFirst**, and then click **Save**.

j. Exit Outlook. Based on your instructor's directions, submit:
out01p3TasksList_LastFirst
out01p3NotesList_LastFirst

Mid-Level Exercises

1 The Home Buyer

You and your significant other are talking about purchasing a home. You have met with some realtors, visited some open houses, and talked to the loan manager at the bank. One day on your way to school, you notice a new For Sale sign in front of a perfect little bungalow. The sign gives the realtor's email address, which you quickly jot down at the next stoplight. You will send an email message enquiring about the listing price of the house, the number of bedrooms and baths, and the size of the lot. You will also ask about the school district and the annual taxes. Once you have gathered the information about the home, you will surprise your significant other by sending an email message describing the home.

a. Begin a new email message in Outlook.
b. Address the message using your email address.
c. Type **out01m1House_LastFirst** for the subject. Mark the message as **High Importance**.
d. Type the following message:

> I am interested in the home that you have listed at 568 Market Avenue. What is the asking price of the property? How many bedrooms and baths? What is the size of the lot? What is the school district? What is the yearly tax assessment?
>
> **Thank you for your time,**
>
> *Your Name*

e. Delete any signature that displays on the message. Send the message. Wait a few minutes, and retrieve the message from the mail server.

DISCOVER
Barbara Stover

f. Set up a Quick Step named **Home Buying**, which moves an email message to a folder in the Inbox called *New Home* when you click the Quick Step. Each time you receive a message related to this exercise, move it to the New Home folder using the Quick Step.

g. Reply to the message as if you were the realtor. Create a signature named **Realtor**, with the text **Agent, Lindenville Homes**. Type the following message in response, adding the signature at the end of the message:

> **Thank you for your interest in the Market Avenue property. I have attached a Word document that gives you the details you requested and more. You may also see the information online at www.LindenvilleHomes.com. Please do not hesitate to call me or send another email if you would like to tour this home.**
>
> **Thank you,**
>
> **Norton Farmer**

h. Attach the file *out01m1MarketAvenue* to the message, and send it. Wait a few minutes, and retrieve the message from the mail server.

i. Open the message, open the attachment, review it, and then close it. Forward the message to your instructor. Make it a high-importance message and Cc yourself. Type this note at the top:

> **I found this super house on the way to school. Want to take a look this weekend?**

j. Send the message, wait a few minutes, and retrieve the message from the mail server. Mark the message for follow up **Tomorrow**.

k. Use the Snipping Tool to take a screenshot of the message list, Folder Pane, and the Task List showing the follow up task. (Hint: Display the To-Do Bar on the Mail Component.) Name the file **out01m1House_LastFirst**.

l. Exit Outlook. Based on your instructor's directions, submit out01m1House_LastFirst.

2 Work Schedule Calendar

As the daytime nursing supervisor at the local hospital, it is your responsibility to schedule nurses so that you have full coverage of the pulmonary wing. You supervise 18 nurses in 2 halls. You decide to create a Work Schedule Calendar for the East Hall for the coming week. Someone else supervises the night staff, so you have to schedule only the daytime hours for the full week. Six people normally work 12-hour shifts on this hall, starting at 8 AM, with two people on duty at a time. One of your nurses is on vacation this week, so the schedules of the remaining five will be displayed on the calendar. To make things interesting, you color-code the calendar, put it in a folder called East Hall, and mark 1-hour lunch breaks so that at least one person is covering the hall at all times. You will create a PDF file to submit to the hospital manager.

a. Start Outlook.

DISCOVER

b. Open the Calendar component, click the Folder tab, and then create a new calendar called **East Hall** in the Calendar folder. Select only the **East Hall calendar** in the Folder Pane to display the East Hall calendar.

c. Set up conditional formatting so that when each nurse's name is in the Subject line, the color-categorization is made automatically. Refer to the table for the color codes.

d. Advance the Calendar to display next week and create a schedule as follows:

Nurse (color-coded category)	Day	Lunch Break
Leslie (Teal)	Monday, Wednesday, Friday	1 PM on Monday, 2 PM on Wednesday, and 1 PM on Friday
Larry (Purple)	Tuesday, Thursday, Sunday	1 PM on Tuesday, 2 PM on Thursday, and 2 PM on Sunday
Marylyn (Orange)	Tuesday, Thursday, Saturday	2 PM on Tuesday, 1 PM on Thursday, and 2 PM on Saturday
Carolyn (Maroon)	Friday, Saturday	2 PM on Friday, 1 PM on Saturday
Marcee (Dark Green)	Monday, Wednesday, Sunday	2 PM on Monday, 1 PM on Wednesday, and 1 PM on Sunday

e. Print the calendar **Weekly Agenda Style** as a Microsoft Print to PDF file. Change the Print Options to display Sunday as the Start Print range, and Saturday as the End Print range. Name the file **out01m2Schedule_LastFirst**.

f. Email the calendar to your instructor using the **Full details** setting, only the dates that were used in this calendar, and attaching the out01m3Schedule_LastFirst file to the message. Use the subject **out01m2CalendarShare_LastFirst**. Remove any signature that appears in the message content prior to sending it.

g. Exit Outlook.

3 Retail Task List

As a manager of a small retail store at the mall, you are responsible for training employees in procedures for closing the store at the end of the day. Many tasks need to be completed, and it is possible that things will be forgotten. To solve this problem, you create a task list that can be used each evening. Because all of the tasks must be completed, you do not set Due Dates for any of them, but you do create categories.

DISCOVER

a. Start Outlook. Click Tasks on the Folder Pane, and click the View tab.
b. Customize the Simple List View Settings so that only the Complete, Subject, Notes, and Categories fields are shown.
c. Create the following tasks, assigning the Showroom tasks the color **Dark Teal** and the Register tasks the color **Steel**:

Subject	Notes	Category
Lock front door	Do not lock door before 9 PM	Showroom
Tidy display shelves		Showroom
Arrange hanging merchandise	All garments facing the same direction, sized correctly	Showroom
Vacuum showroom	Empty dust container afterwards	Showroom
Run register tapes	Keystrokes: CTR+REG, Click today's date	Register
Count receipts	Note number of each denomination	Register
Lock change in register	$25 in ones, $50 in fives, $50 in tens, $60 in twenties	Register
Lock excess money in safe		Register
Arm the alarm	Code: SET+4392	Showroom
Lock back door	Outside code: 2839	Showroom

d. Adjust the widths of the columns so that all of the entries can be viewed completely in Simple List view. Sort the list by category.
e. Print the task list in **Table Style** as a Microsoft Print to PDF file named **out01m3Showroom_LastFirst**.
f. Exit Outlook. Based on your instructor's directions, submit out01m3Showroom_LastFirst.

Beyond the Classroom

Astronomy Calendar

GENERAL CASE

As the newsletter editor for the local astronomy club, you are responsible for getting the word out to the members about astronomical events that will be occurring each month. Using online research, develop the sky events calendar with at least 10 events for the coming month. Use more than one resource to develop the calendar and make notes using Outlook to keep track of the information. In the message portion of each calendar appointment, record the source of your information (e.g., the Web site) and any important information, such as how someone would identify the sky event. Print the calendar in Calendar Details Style as a PDF file named **out01b1Astronomy_LastFirst** so that it can be included in the next newsletter mailing. Based on your instructor's directions, submit out01b1Astronomy_LastFirst.

The Wedding Planner

DISASTER RECOVERY

Your sister is soon to be married. One afternoon you sit down to hear about the wedding plans, only to discover that every scrap of information that has been gathered to this point is just that—a scrap of paper. Sensing a real disaster about to happen, you offer to develop a contact list and a Contact Group for email messages to the bridal party (three bridesmaids and three groomsmen), calendar, and task list, using Outlook. Think of it as your gift to the bride, who will be much calmer because of your planning. Send an email message to your sister (use your instructor's email address and the subject line **out01b2Wedding_LastFirst**) to tell her about everything you plan to do in the electronic format. Create a calendar with at least five appointments for the wedding date, fittings for the gown, bachelorette party, rehearsal dinner, and so on. Develop a Contact Group that contains the names and email addresses of the six people (bridesmaids and groomsmen) who will be in the wedding party. Create Contacts with at least five commonly used services for a wedding, such as caterer, reception hall, minister, and tux shop. As you put together the task list with at least five tasks, remember that tasks might have ending dates, but they are not scheduled events like calendar items, so if you need an appointment to complete the task, like you might to meet with caterers, it is not a task but a calendar event. Apply categories and conditional formatting, and customize the views of the information to make it easy to understand. Print a PDF copy of the calendar (named **out01b2WeddingCalendar_LastFirst**), contact list (named **out01b2WeddingContacts_LastFirst**), and task list in an appropriate style (named **out01b2WeddingTasks_LastFirst**). Based on your instructor's directions, submit the following:

out01b2WeddingCalendar_LastFirst
out01b2WeddingContacts_LastFirst
out01b2WeddingTasks_LastFirst

Capstone Exercise

The Student Resource Center at your school has a robust tutoring/mentoring program. Students who serve as tutors are paid by the hour. Mentoring is done on a volunteer basis, but many of the students who are tutors are also mentors. The services are free to the students needing help with their coursework or in the adjustment to academic life. You have been tutoring for about six weeks and recently volunteered as a mentor. Your schedule is getting hectic and you have lots of reasons for needing an assistant, so you turn to Outlook to help organize your schedule, maintain a contact list for the students that you tutor, and to send email.

Contacts List Setup

You are currently tutoring four students. You begin by setting up the contact information for them.

a. Add these contacts to Outlook:

Student Name	Email Address	Phone (Note: All phone numbers are for mobile phones)	Notes
John Meyers	JMeyersStudent@outlook.com	321-555-2938	COMP150
Steve Bailey	StevenBStudent@school.edu	321-555-2397	COMP190
Sung Ye	SYeStudent@school.edu	321-555-5843	COMP190
Anil Datta	AnilDattaStudent@school.edu	321-555-4736	Mentoring

b. Create a Contact Group called **COMP150** that contains the people in COMP150 that you tutor. Add **your contact information** to the COMP150 group.

c. Change to the List view. (Note: You may have to click Reset View in order to see the contacts.) Customize the View Settings by showing only the fields that contain information. The fields should appear in the same order as shown in the table from Step a. Make any adjustments to the field widths to show the full contents of each field.

d. Print the phone list in **Table Style** as a PDF file named **out01c1TutorContacts_LastFirst**.

Calendar

Using the Calendar, you will schedule your classes, tutoring, and mentoring appointments.

a. Add a new calendar called **Tutoring**, and move to the Week calendar for next week.

b. Schedule the following classes on the calendar:

COMP200	Monday–Wednesday 8–10 AM
PSYC340	Tuesday and Thursday 11 AM–1 PM
BUSM350	Monday and Friday 1–3 PM

c. Schedule the following tutoring/mentoring sessions. Set a reminder of a half of an hour prior to each:

COMP150	Wednesday 4–5 PM
COMP190	Thursday 3–5 PM
Mentoring	Tuesday 2–3 PM

d. Create conditional formatting rules in the Calendar view that show any mention of COMP150 in the color-coded category **Dark Purple**, COMP190 in **Dark Blue**, and Mentoring in **Dark Red**.

e. Display the calendar in Week view, and take a screenshot. Name the file **out01c1Calendar_LastFirst**.

Tasks and Notes

As a busy student, you need to keep track of your tasks so that you get your own work done as well as prepare for the tutoring appointments.

a. Create a new folder in My Tasks called **School Tasks**. Put the following tasks into the folder:

Subject	Start Date	Notes
COMP150	Tuesday	Check with instructor regarding Boolean searches.
PSYC340	Monday	Complete experiment.
PSYC340	Monday	Put down some ideas for final project.
Mentoring	Tuesday	Find out if Kathy can meet on weekends.
COMP200	Thursday	Study for midterm.

b. Return to the Calendar view, select next week, and then print a Tri-fold Style calendar showing the calendar and the tasks for Tuesday only, as a PDF file named **out01c1Calendar_LastFirst**.

c. Create a note titled **Final project requirements**, with the following text: **4–6 pages, double-spaced. Include Executive Summary. Headings should be bold and larger than rest of text. References are shown on a separate page.**

d. Print the note in Memo Style as a PDF file named **out01c1Note_LastFirst**.

Email

You have found that sending out reminders regarding tutoring appointments is very helpful in getting students to show up for their appointments.

a. Create a folder in the email Inbox called **Tutoring**. All of the mail related to tutoring and mentoring will be stored here.

b. Move to the Calendar for next week. Drag the **COMP150 tutoring appointment** to the Mail icon on the Folder Pane to open the email client and place the calendar entry into the message.

c. Select the **COMP150 Contact Group** for the To box. Change the Subject to **out01c1COMP150_LastFirst**.

d. Type this in the message: **Can you make it to this tutoring session on Wednesday? Thanks,** *Your Name*.

e. Create a signature named **Mentor**, with your name and **Mentor, Student Resource Center** as the text of the signature. Add the signature to the message.

f. Send the message, wait a few minutes, and then retrieve the message from the mail server.

g. Open the message and reply with: **I can be there. Can you give me a website to review where I can read more about Microsoft OneNote? I will see you on Wednesday in the Tutoring Center. Bye, John**.

h. Send the message, wait a few minutes, and then retrieve the message from the mail server.

i. Forward the message to your instructor with this message: **As you can see, I will be meeting with John Meyers on Wednesday. Would it be acceptable to you to suggest the website of www.office.microsoft.com/onenote? Thank you,** *Your Name*. Add the Mentor Signature before you send the message, modify the subject to include **FW:out01c1ForwardMessage_LastFirst**. Use the Cc field to send the message to your email address as well.

j. Send the message, wait a few minutes, and then retrieve the message from the mail server.

k. Print the message you just received in **Memo Style** Microsoft Print to PDF file named **out01c1Message_LastFirst**. It will show the progression of messages.

l. Drag all email related to the tutoring exercise into the Tutoring folder. Open the Tutoring Folder to display the email messages in the message list, and take a screenshot to show the Folder Pane and the message list. Name the file **out01c1TutoringFolder_LastFirst**.

m. Exit Outlook. Based on your instructor's directions, submit:

out01c1TutorContacts_LastFirst
out01c1Calendar_LastFirst
out01c1Note_LastFirst
out01c1Message_Lastfirst
out01c1TutoringFolder_LastFirst

Glossary

Appointment A block of time where other people or resources are not scheduled.

Attached file A file created in a software application that is appended to an email message for transmission to the recipient. When received, the file can be opened using the appropriate software or saved to the local computer.

Category An organizational feature that enables you to color-code and name groups of email, appointments, contacts, or tasks. This groups like items together for easy retrieval.

Conditional formatting A process of setting up rules applied to appointments, contacts, or tasks to make them stand out from other items.

Conversation A group of messages that share the same subject line and appear together with graphics indicating the relationship between the messages. Your replies to messages are shown, as well as the messages you received.

Date Navigator A monthly calendar, shown in the Navigation Pane, which can be used to select a date for display on the calendar.

Deleted Items folder A recycle bin that contains email that you have deleted. Messages stay in the Deleted Items folder until you empty the folder or delete an item individually.

Drafts folder A folder that stores email which has been saved but not sent. You can click the Save icon as you compose a long message to save it to this folder. Most often, draft messages are saved as you navigate away from the message window.

Folder Pane A pane on the Outlook window that contains folders, calendars, and buttons for organizing information for each of the components of Outlook.

Inbox A default folder that receives incoming email.

Junk Email folder A folder that contains messages identified as possible spam by the Junk Email Filter. This folder should be viewed regularly and unneeded messages deleted.

Mail client A program such as Microsoft Outlook 2016 on your computer or a web-based application such as Outlook.com that enables you to compose, send, and receive email messages.

Mail server A special-purpose computer with an Internet connection such as you might have in your campus computer network, or it is a computer at your Internet Service Provider such as Verizon, Comcast, or your cable company. The mail server functions as a central post office and provides private mailboxes to people authorized to use its services.

Meeting An event scheduled with one or more attendees for whom Outlook will automatically create and send email notifications.

Netiquette Etiquette rules for the Internet and a group of commonly accepted good practices. Most often, this applies to email.

Outbox folder A folder that contains all of the messages you have written that have not yet been uploaded to the server. When you connect to the server, these messages will automatically be transferred to the server.

Quick Step Multiple commands compressed into a single click accessed from the Ribbon of the Mail component of Outlook.

Reading Pane The portion of the Outlook window that displays the text of a selected message, appointment, contact, or task. The Reading Pane can appear on the right or bottom of the window. It can also be turned off.

Rule A method of automatically managing incoming email by applying steps, such as moving messages to a specified folder, playing a sound, or displaying in a New Item Alert window based on criteria, as a message is received.

Sent Items folder A folder that contains copies of messages that have been uploaded to the mail server.

To-Do Bar A pane on the right side of the Outlook window that provides a quick overview of the calendar, upcoming appointments, and tasks. It is visible whenever the calendar component is not displayed. It can be minimized or expanded.

Index

Italics indicate illustrations, tables, sidebars, or photos.

A

address book. *See* Contacts
appointments. *See* Calendar
appropriate language, *15*
attachments, 13, *15*, 16

B

backup, creating, *34*
blind carbon copy (Bcc), 13, *13*, *14*

C

Calendar
   managing, 42–45, *42*, *43*, *44*, *45*
   view appointments with, 7, *7*
carbon/courtesy copy (Cc), 13, *13*, *14*
components, Outlook, 4–9, *5*, *6*, *7*, *8*
   synergism of, *6*
conditional formatting, 44, *44*
Contacts, 7, *8*
   managing, *30*, 30–34, *31*, *32*, *33*, *34*
conversations, 11–12, *12*

D

Date Navigator, *42*, *43*
Deleted Items folder, 12
deleting entries, 47
Desktop client, *4*

E

email, 5, 9–19. *See also* Inbox
   creating a message, 12–14, *13*, *14*, *15*
   printing, 16
   privacy, lack of, *12*
   replying to or forwarding, 15, *16*
   signature, 16–17, *17*
   viewing, 5–6, *6*
   working with other email clients, *4*
Exchange server, 9, 11, 45

F

Favorites, 5–6
Folder Pane, 5, *5*, 8
folders, email, *17*, 17–19, *18*, *19*
follow up, marking for, 19

H

help, 9

I

Inbox, 6, *6*
   managing, *10*, 10–12, *11*, *12*
integration of components, *6*
Internet Access Message Protocol (IMAP), 9

J

Junk Email folder, 17, *17*

L

Layout group, 5, *5*

M

mail client, 9
mail server, 9
Map It, *30*
meetings. *See* Calendar
Mentions, *14*
message list commands, *11*
Message Preview, *6*

N

Navigation Options, 5
Netiquette, 14, *15*
Notes, adding, 47, *47*

O

OneNote, 19, *19*
Outlook.com, *4*
   synchronizing with Outlook, 9

P

password, 10, *10*
People, 7
People icon, 6, *6*, 31, *31*
Personal Folders, 5–6
Post Office Protocol (POP3), 9, 11
printing e-mails, 16

Q

Quick Steps, 18–19, *19*

R

Reading Pane, 6, *6*, 10, *10*
   previewing attachments in, 16
Ribbon, 4
rules, setting up, 18, *18*, 44

S

searching
   Web, 9
   Smart Lookup, 9
stationery, adding, 14
synergism among components, *6*

T

task buttons, changing the order, 5
Tasks, *8*, 8–9
   managing, 45–46, *46*
To-Do Bar. *See* Tasks
To-Do List. *See* Tasks

U

username, 10

V

View tab, 5, *5*